To Mary,

Eva McLelland
2008

Restless Winds

Restless Winds

Eva McLelland

VANTAGE PRESS
New York

FIRST EDITION

All rights reserved, including the right of
reproduction in whole or in part in any form.

Copyright © 2003 by Eva McLelland

Published by Vantage Press, Inc.
516 West 34th Street, New York, New York 10001

Manufactured in the United States of America
ISBN: 0-533-14423-X

Library of Congress Catalog Card No.: 2002094200

0 9 8 7 6 5 4 3 2 1

To Brig. Gen. Mark Musick, whose assistance has been a great inspiration

Contents

Ages of Time	1
Adversities vs. Musical Crescendos	2
Ages of Decadence	3
A Flash at a Time	4
Age of Innocence	5
A Little Country Church	6
A Maiden's Sweet Dream	7
A Mural in Mid-Air	8
Angels to the Rescue	10
Animated Shadows	11
A Poet's Dream	12
Appointment with the Birds	13
A Rarity Supreme	14
As Day and Night Blend	15
As Nature Decrees	16
A Splendorous Sunrise	17
Autumn Cycle	18
Autumn's Threshold	19
A Writer to Be	20
Barren Dignity	21
Beauty All But Gone	22
Bedtime	23
Bits and Pieces of a Soul	24
Blessings of Faith	25
Blessings of the Sea	26
Boulevard of Broken Dreams	27
Breathlessly Beautiful	28
Change of Station	29
Childhood Inspirations	30

Childhood Recollections	31
Cimarron	32
Clemency	33
Color on the Old Smokehouse	34
Contemporary Traffic Compared to Old Days	35
Crescent on High	37
Crossroads of Life	38
Crying Out at Night	39
Dawning of the Morning	40
Days of the Best	41
Dazzling Sunrise	42
Destiny	43
Diamond Trees	44
Doors of Reverie	45
Dream Castles	46
Dream World Kingdom	47
Each Day, Thankful Be	48
Early Morning Blessings	49
Early Morning Thoughts	50
Earth Angel	51
Efforts and Burdens	52
Embers of the Past	53
Evening Peace	54
Evening Prayer	55
Extant Celestial Glory	56
Extension of Time	57
Eyes of Stars	58
Fascinating Creatures	59
Fiery Imagination	60
"Flame of Life"	61
Flecks of Reflection	62
Freddy, My Angel	63
Friendship, a Treasure	64
Fretful Clouds	65
From Whence, A Bard!	66
Friend Whippoorwill	67
Freaks of Nature	68

Faith	69
Genealogy of the Trees	70
Gentle Winds	72
Glory of a Storm	73
Glowing Tones	74
Goals and Dilemmas	75
God's Gemstones	77
Golden Moments	78
Gone Are the Simple Days	79
Grandmother's Advice	80
Great Colors of Autumn	81
Great Wonders	82
Haiku	83
Halls of Wisdom	84
Healing Manifestations	85
Heavenly Array	86
Heavenly Creatures Up in a Tree	87
His Omnipresence	88
Humble Wordage	89
Imprisonment in a Cocoon	90
In Quest for Affection	91
Joys of Yesteryears—Today's New Sorrows	92
Kaleidoscopic Glow	93
Last Thoughts of the Day	94
Leaves Hanging On	95
Life	96
Lifelong Quest	97
Life Force Enfolded	98
Like a Distant Star	99
Little Creatures	100
Lost in the Wilderness	101
Lost Soulmate	102
Love's Sweet Blessings	103
Love's Sweet Victory	104
Magnificent Manifestations	105
Mama	106
Meditations	107

Memories of Old	108
Metaphoric Sounds	109
Miracles of Nature	110
Miss Sensation of the Waves	111
Molly	112
Moonrise	114
Moonset	115
Moonship	116
Most Beautiful Time of the Year	117
Mural of All Murals	118
Musical Serenity	119
My Creature Kingdom	120
My Friends, the Wrens	121
My Mark in Music	122
My Peace	123
My Prayer	124
My River	126
My Sands of Time	127
Nature's Diamonds	128
Nature's Free Beauty	129
Nature's Gems	130
Nature's Life	131
Nick (NK)	132
Night Sounds	133
November '99	134
Oak Creek Canyon	135
One Yesterday	136
On Wings of an Eagle	137
Passage of Time	138
Peace and Silence	139
Performance of the Trees	140
Phenomena of Three	141
Phenomenal Transitions	142
Picturesque	143
Playhouse Sites	144
Plea for Existence	145
Poetry in a Sack	146

Precious Life	147
Predestination	148
Pre-Planned Existence	149
Queen of the Sky	150
Quietly, Dawn Is Breaking	151
Rainy Season in Dothan, Alabama	152
Ratio and Proportion	153
Ratio to Appreciation	154
Reclamation	155
Rhapsodic Musing	156
Rhapsody	157
Rhymes of Gold in Ages of Gray	158
Rhymes in Dreams	159
Rose of My Heart	160
Rustic Scenes of Nature	161
Sacred Vows	162
Sans Freedom	163
Second Childhood	164
Save the Trees	165
Scorn of a Storm	166
Sensational Vibrations	167
Sensational Winds	169
Sequel to the Gypsy Violinist	170
She Sleeps in Peace	171
Silence of Morning	172
Sky of Splendor	173
So in Love	174
Soulmates	175
Space	176
Spectrums of Wonder	177
Stark and Staunch, the Trees	178
Stringy Little Tree	179
Sunset and Twilight	180
Sunset at Its Best	181
Sir Woody	182
Simultaneous Phenomena	183
Syncopated Rhythm	184

Time	185
Talking to the Moon	186
The Active Little Leaf	187
The Baby Oak Tree	188
The Bounty	189
The Breeze and the Trees	190
The Cedarwood Heart	191
The Coming of the Green	192
The Eagle's Prey	193
The Enchanting Storm	194
The Fennel and the Goldenrod	195
The Three Fennels	196
The Fiddling Man	198
The Final Glory	200
The General and the Private	201
The Glory of Shadows	202
The Good Old Days	203
The Gypsy Violinist	204
The Lady and Her Flute	205
The Little Fennel Seed	206
The Little Switch Tree and What It Grew Up to Be	207
The Lonely Tree	208
The Mangled Little Oak	209
The Master's Brush	210
The Mighty Storm	211
The Mills of the Gods	212
The Old Ghost Town	213
The Orange Rose	214
To an Orange Rose	215
The Last Orange Rose	216
The Old Oak Tree Above the Eaves	217
The Power of Reflection	218
The Ruby in the Sky	219
The Scribbler	220
The Sounds of Night	221
The Story in My Heart	222

The Sun Bids Adieu	223
The Touch of His Hand	224
The Unawakened Forest	225
The Wise Old Oak	226
The Unveiling	227
The Voice of Silence	228
The Whole World a Canvas	229
The Wonderful Field of Medicine	230
Things Unforetold	231
Thoughts from Afar	232
Thwarted Realms of Time	233
Timeless Beauty	234
Time for Rest	235
To Each His Own	237
To Forever Abide	238
To Fulfill Unfinished Efforts	239
To Like the Eagle, Be	240
To Paint a Word Picture	241
Tree and Bird Story	242
Two Proud Little Leaves	244
Unacclaimed Lines	245
Undulating Patterns	246
Unfinished Endeavors	247
Unmended Fences	248
Voices in the Wind	249
Wayward Winds	250
Window View of Beauty	251
Wishful Dreams of Heaven	252
Wonderful Wonders	253
Wonderful Words of Rhyme	254
Words Gone Adrift	255
Yearning for Learning	256

Restless Winds

Ages of Time

With cloudbursts of sunshine alighting on the roof,
   How could any poet dare remain aloof?
These things, and more, make a great combination
   To invest in my soul-inspiring great vibrations!

Long rays of light shine down through the trees,
With mystic bits of rhythm—voices drifting on the
   breeze.
And murmurs of a brook trickling down through the
   ravine—
All take me back to where it's time to sit and dream.

   Glory is drifting through the trees of time—
     Invented forests, and events sublime,
  From imaginative memories going back in ages,
Encapsulating with dust, the words of ancient sages.

  Wake me not, oh, voices of contemporary existence.
 Remind me not that there's a question of subsistence.
    I'll stay as I am until the ages of time
   Take away my ability to make a verse rhyme.

Adversities vs. Musical Crescendos

Through shadows of life
    midst struggle and strife,
Adversities keep rolling along,
    just merrily singing their song.

Ne'er 'tis mercy as need be known,
And naught 'tis pity to be shown.
Yet in early morning light
When I've passed safely through the night,
Crescendos of music come cascading all around,
With glorious swelling of the sound,
As a flower being released from a seed in the ground.

Through this sensation of being
    I am brought to be seeing
That there must be a new beginning,
As if, in a cocoon, I am spinning—
A labyrinth to follow,
    new teachings to borrow,
From which there shall be no sorrow.

Ages of Decadence

Waiting for I know not what—
Perhaps to better make my lot,
Via pathways of rugged trail,
Midst enmeshed networks of travail—
Just when the time is meant to be
For revelations clear to me.
I'm mindful then that I am not
Distracted, in a state besot,
With ages of decadence long past—
Sans powerful controls o'er the mast.
Anon 'tis furled, sails shall be,
Unless en masse, we're out to sea!

A Flash at a Time

It's utter futility
      and beyond my ability—
Expressing my feelings in full detail;
Phrases for me now are but frail—
Insufficient for showing justice,
      thus to entail
Awaiting further opportunity
To gain a continuation
      of absorbing inspiration
For writing verses of import,
Worthy of media's next report.
Sometimes I wrack my brain in vain,
      further to complain
That inspiration is all gone,
      and as I sit here alone,
I reminisce of days before,
When I thought 'twas then all o'er.
But later on, in a flash at a time,
A line or two would fall into rhyme.
I hope always to regain
      and that 'twill not be bane,
But (just as before)
      phrases will all come out the same.

Age of Innocence

In her Easter Bonnet
        she was a vivid sonnet—
Dimpled cheeks, turned-up nose,
All new outfit, from head to toes!
Dancing eyes (laughing too),
Flashing tones of green and blue.
Charisma, yes, she's loaded with this!
Her every experience, to her, is bliss!
Her age of innocence is something rare—
A treasure to be held with greatest of care.
'Tis sad to think how, come what may,
That soon this innocence could be cast away,
Ne'er to return another day!

A Little Country Church

A little country church with a steeple
Is a memory of long ago;
And what a variety of many, many people
(All different personae) through my thoughts now flow!

The most interesting part of the day
Was gathering in the churchyard
To pass the time away—
Just waiting to see who'd be the lucky one,
Chosen by the preacher for this day of fun.

After a lunch of fried chicken, peas and rice,
And games for kiddies, who'd been so nice,
The rest of the day passed fast away,
And then 'tis time again to pray.

Back to church at beginning of night—
Organ notes softly pealing, ethereally quiet—
A perfect preparation
For once more, a week's cessation.

A Maiden's Sweet Dream

A few little words that rhyme,
When arranged in three-quarter time,
Become a maiden's sweet dream,
With delight, supreme,

As she glides in her darling's arms,
Listening to his words of charm—
Round and round,
With a toe-tapping sound,

On a floor that seems made of glass,
Reflections emoting elegance and class;
To a waltz, more than justice can he
Do, accompanied by a lass such as she.

A Mural in Mid-Air

How simply can this I say,
"It gets prettier every day!"
Can you imagine a mural
    being painted in mid-air?
Without even a ladder or a stair?
Perfectly-matched patterns
    and colors, so fair—
Painted with all ease,
    of nature's care.
My whole existence is
    created out there.
Nature is my sustenance,
    my reason for living.
Without it, I'd have nothing
    of worth for giving
Back to God's creations,
    from whence I came.
Little can I give, for the world's gain,
But humbly glad I am
    to give what I can.
Without vision of sight,
    life would be a sad plight.
The wonders of nature
    are what I live by.
Without this inspiration,
    I surely would die.
So I pray, dear Jesus, for more time to create,
    and power to articulate
What I feel inside,

Which for so long I've tried
    to bring outside
For the world to see
    what's motivating me.

Angels to the Rescue

Life has been a melody of love,
Direct from a power up above.
Angels are on earth, so they say—
Confirmation of which, if I may,
For many a time have I been
On the brink of disaster
      when God would send
An angel to rescue me
From what (fate only
      knows) was to be.
Now, Jesus, I pray, please,
      protection, to me, give,
That for longer may I live,
To strengthen and portray talent
      with which I'm blest,
With each manifestation
      at Thy behest.

Animated Shadows

Animated shadows dance upon the floor
    just beyond the door,
Where mini-blinds admit the light,
Coming through the window, and
    shining through the night.

This kaleidoscopic movement, I could
    watch here all night long—
To hear the crickets chirping, and the
    whippoorwill's night song.

'Twould be so very sweet
    if, like the birds,
        I'd go "Tweet, tweet!"
Flying high and all around,
    then come down,
        back to the ground—

And run inside to check
    moving patterns on the floor
Which, I discover, are no more,
Except one tiny little speck.

A Poet's Dream

She stood, captured,
And totally enraptured
By molten heaps of melted-away love—
Collections of emotions
That had, since childhood, become promotions
Toward the dream of her life
(Midst struggle and strife).
There stood her statue, beside Old Glory,
Anxious to tell the story,
Of how she climbed the hill to victory,
Albeit through feats so contradictory,
To attain Poet Laureate of the World—
Glorious banners, all unfurled!
Oh, dear Jesus, a pity it's to be
Only a dream! Sad is she!

Appointment with the Birds

From their secret bowers,
Birds come in showers,
From surrounding treetops,
    all around,
Descending to a favorite spot
    on the ground,
Where the grand old oak,
    sweetgum, and pine,
Surrounding, to keep
    the birds in line,
With their scheduled convergence
To attend this occurrence
Of their daily appointment with
    the "lady of the birds."
Can she, or can she not, be the
    "Queen of the Nerds?"
"No matter," said she, "for I'll
    always be
In love with the birds from
    here to eternity."

A Rarity Supreme

Through the branches of a tree,
    a shaft of light
        shone down on me.
The purity of the moonbeam
    is a rarity, supreme,
Considering its source,
    and periodic course
As nightly it traverses the sky,
    its beauty on the world to ply.
From my little watch groove,
    I am hesitant to move,
Lest the splendor would escape,
    and my inspiration, take!
Awake! For tonight you've much to say
    before the break of day.
Pick up your quill
    before daylight the awe may spill!

In blissful silence, I watched daylight
    overtake the moon,
And in the blink of an eye,
    it all occurred so soon!

As Day and Night Blend

At the setting of the sun
My work is not yet done—
No, 'tis just about now to begin,
Right about now, at the day's end—

I'd like to go out
        and ramble about,
To observe the approach of darkness,
In all of its awesome starkness,
As day and night begin to blend.
'Tis obvious to me that these phenomena
        never end.

The blazing sun is doing its best
As it commands the world, at its behest:
"Wait for me—I'll return to thee,
In all my glory—you shall see!"

As Nature Decrees

Stark and naked are the trees,
As nature now decrees.
Low sets the sun, with colors all aglow—
Wisps of feathery clouds, all in a row.

Look to the east, where first the color blends—
Then to the west, where last the daylight ends.
Long strands of sunbeams piercing through the trees,
With alternating shadows cooling half the breeze.

A Splendorous Sunrise

Watching strata of glory fade away
To the beginning of another day,
With mutation of colors just past—
Grandiloquence of wonders cast,
To vivid tones, through just one glance,
Like the striking hues of a wild Flamenco Dance
Changing to the sweetness of a baby's soft kiss,
In the early morning mist,
Bringing to sudden realization
The omnipotent magnificence of all creation!

Autumn Cycle

When I look out across the rooftop
    of the house across the way,
Webster's insufficient to explain
    what I have to say!
Strata and strata of color,
    from autumn's blessed gift,
Have all been scattered out,
    and then set adrift.
"Oh, Mr. Neighbor, please
    don't clear your roof—
But please allow some precious leaves
    to remain up there, aloof!
I'll run and fetch my camera, and
    when developed, you'll see proof
That you have the prettiest housetop—
And for lookers-on, 'twill be non-stop,
Throughout a beautiful day—
As nature's on its way!"

Autumn's Threshold

Looking out the window, I'm speechless in wonder,
And my heart is cut asunder
From the beauty I behold
      on this autumn's great threshold.
Of all seasons seen before,
'Tis unequaled, heretofore.
If I die now, it's from duress
From inability to express—
For no words, or no brushes
Portray how spirit to my heart rushes.
I cannot leave the window,
      nor must I stop to eat,
For the beauty of this moment
      ne'er can time repeat.
If I leave for just one moment,
      opportunity will have fled,
For the sun, in its orbit,
      will have moved overhead,
Bringing forth the shadows,
      to obscure the colors there.
And I'll have only sorrow
      to spread everywhere.
So let me take my pen and write while I may
Of all the awe and wonder
      of this great and glorious day!

A Writer to Be

When I retreat to my cozy little lair,
No one knows that I'm there.
I curl in my cocoon
And write till way past noon.

While others are still abed,
The sun sweeps treetops o'er head.
Depth of richness in color and beauty
Never before having been approached,
Albeit, by some, were efforts to have encroached.

Inspiration, overwhelming, emanates from the ground,
Where gold and green leaves are spread all around.
Such splendor ne'er before, nor has there been since—
Nay, none by artists, nor in prints.

God willed the day that I should stay
Sufficiently long to witness the birth
Of such phenomena this great, here on earth!

Impact on speech, much to be quelled
From glory of splendor and color, unexcelled—
Lord, give me the blessed ability
To gain full peace from this tranquility.

Barren Dignity

Now the trees, most bare,
Have a dignity so rare.
The task they face from here
Will include what they do to prepare
For the next oncoming year.
There are leaves so distributed
    to enrich the good earth soil,
Carefully sifting all the seeds
    so as not to foil
Preservation, of which
    ensures future existence—
And a few left for the birds
    with hunger and persistence.
Albeit harried by strong winds,
    yet with elegant grandiosity,
Stands the great old oak
    of famed philosophy,
Its branches reaching out,
    as if to implore,
(Beset by sad experiences
    that have gone on before):
"Please do not rake my leaves
    and acorns, galore;
They are here for nature's purpose,
    and to destroy them, I abhor!
If you break the cycles of nature,
    you'll not have some pictures to store,
Of all God's colorful creations,
For your future generations."

Beauty All But Gone

> Shalt once you see
> For thee and me
> 'Tis wont to be
> Forever more mine angst
> That gone is beauty from reserve,
> Bounty of life for to observe,
> Once all mine, for the asking—
> 'Tis naught now but for tasking.

To think my seeing, most all flown,
Leaves beauty of life all but gone.
Pray, God, don't take it all from me—
More than just shadows, could it not be?

Bedtime

Now as I put myself to bed,
All misgivings must I shed.
I leave my worries a while tonight
While I turn out the light
And say my prayer,
And cast aside my every care.
Can I but find it in my heart
With every vengeful thought to part—
I pray that God will find a way
To erase each ugly thought each day.
And now my soul I pray He'll keep
As I lay me down to sleep.

Bits and Pieces of a Soul

She was not the Alice in a land of wonder,
But, to bits and pieces, was torn asunder—
One piece here,
Another bit there,
Living in a dream world far from home,
Enveloped by realms from whichever to roam
Through strata of grandeur, past gates of pearl.
Faster and faster, did her thoughts e'er whirl,
With wings of ether in lightness she'd ascend,
Surely, in likeness of angels, in trend.
She practiced, ever daily, how she'd curtsy
                                  to His Grace,
In hopes she'd see Mother, face to face—
And Grandmother, too, (if good she had been),
Both champions to her cause, and her best friends.
She said, "Lord, if it's not asking too much,
May I see my precious pets and give them a touch?
That's all I would ask
In exchange for all burdens I've taken
                                  as my task."

Blessings of Faith

I was blessed today
    with a renewal of vigor—
Welcome visitors
    made my heart bigger
With faith and love,
    strengthened from above.
Alone was I, groping for trust,
Thinking to die, that I must,
When some missionaries came my way,
To leave and come back another day.
The tranquil peace, they bring, with a smile,
Me, 'twill carry, many a mile.
Vibrations of their spirit
    bring me back to life—
Ne'er more will I
    think of strife.

Blessings of the Sea

Dancing waves sparkled in the moonlight,
As dolphins played all through the night.
Nearest in likeness, to people, they are.
In a swimming performance,
A dolphin is the star,
So endearing to humanity,
Sending waves of vibratory sound,
And thence from man to dolphin—
Like, to each other, they are bound
By understanding beyond measure
In relentless quest of treasure.
Pray, forever, let it be—
Those wonderful blessings of the sea.

Boulevard of Broken Dreams

Living on a boulevard of broken dreams
Isn't very conducive to pleasant scenes,
In a kaleidoscopic cacophony of imaginary things—
A state of mind that living alone brings.

I had it all figured out—
What life was about,
And all I had to do
Was plan ahead a day or two.

Albeit we are wont to aspire,
Happenstances don't always transpire.
Nor do hours of days hold back
Till the dreaded task, we decide to attack.

Life could be so beautiful
Had we no need for dutiful
Fulfillments, or friends to forsake
Through obligations to others we make.

Now back to the boulevard of broken dreams,
And how to avoid complicated schemes.

Breathlessly Beautiful

From the jade of the green of the leaves hanging low,
O'er the earth tones down where dead leaves go,
So charming and divine
My heartstrings did entwine!
So breathlessly was I entranced!
One moment, only, had I just glanced
(My thoughts being only of the day ahead)—
I was shocked by reality of beauty, instead!
If a sample of life on the other side this could be,
Then, Lord, please hurry it on to me!

Change of Station

Seems outside is getting rough,
But glancing out my window,
    things don't look so tough.
My mind reaches out and switches
    off the heat,
In exchange for a station of a
    much lower beat.

A few feet from me,
    out my window I can see
Miracles of nature in every tree.
With every sway of a bough,
    as the wind sweeps through,

And the vastness of the sky,
    in its robin's-egg blue,
Is more than enough departure
    from the present anomaly
To tune out unwelcome speeches from
    the one who punishes me.

Childhood Inspirations

The russet of the cluster on the overhanging bough
(In moments of memory, I recall now),
To my heart brought a thrill,
As I took my seat on the window sill.

In the attic room of our old farm home,
Where I often went to be alone,
Many a tranquil moment I spent,
As over my school book lessons I went,

Making sure each subject would be covered,
As in the chill of the room I hovered,
Observing as I read that the color was changing
In the cluster of leaves which overhead were hanging.

The beauty of nature, absorbed in inspiration,
Gave rise to my share of poetic creation,
While hours of reverie I dreamed away,
Wishing that in childhood I could stay.

Childhood Recollections

Blue of the blue, in skies up above,
And green of the green of trees in my alcove,
Takes me back to times of childhood I love,
When worries were but few
        and my thoughts ran two and two!
Nothing matters so much as a merry little fling,
Up through the air in my grapevine swing!
And then down through the meadow to chase
    butterflies.
But my direction of recollection possibly belies,
Thus maybe ending up picking violets in the glen,
Where I stood in admiration, listening to the wren,
After which I would return to the mother of my heart,
With loving thoughts, which to her,
        I would ever more impart.

Cimarron

The orchestra was playing
    Cimarron—so sweet!
It enlivened the feet
    to rise in premature ovation—
        a most splendid creation!

The conductor bowed
    and applause became loud—
Begging, "Maestro, please!" (by the score)
    "just once more!"
Into mid-air, the baton rose
As fiddlers picked up their bows.
To the words of song,
    fiddles did a fast jiggety-jig!
And the evening's entertainment
    was nothing less than big!

Clemency

There was the clang of the bell in the tower,
Apprising the town of the seventeenth hour.
And the creak of the hinge on the big rusty gate
Was the final note to visitors coming late.
She stood looking through the bars,
Seeking a glimpse of her long-lost son,
As had become her habit when each day was done.
At the finish of her duties,
Before retiring for rest,
She went trudging at her best,
Trying to make it on time,
Hoping to find a warden, benign,
Who would sympathetically add her to the line.
One day a warden, new,
With a heart so kind and true,
Was standing by the gate
When she arrived late.
Noticing the limp in her gait,
One minute, naught, did he hesitate.
As he quickly passed her through,
Life for her began anew,
For only thoughts concerning her boy
Were all her mind could employ.
To make a story short,
Further crime did she abort,
Through exemplary love and care,
Supported by her constant prayer.
And today her son is free,
By God's own decree!

Color on the Old Smokehouse

On an old smokehouse, there's a beam across the end,
From the sun that's shining through,
Accelerating the sound of the whistle of the wind,
And the sky emphasizes the blue.

'Tis color that sets my heart on fire,
And without which there's nothing to inspire
The great things of life I've been reading about,
And for which benefits I'm on the scout.

Matters not what shall be
      if it but pleases me,
With imaginary security I surmise,
In its usual spectacular style,
Tomorrow there shall be
      an awesomely great sunrise!

Contemporary Traffic Compared to Old Days

In great volume,
    falls the sweet night air
        upon me
As I lie by my window,
    the traffic for to hear
        and bright lights for to see.

I wonder where they're going—
    seems not ever they are slowing,
        while whizzin' past—
          so fast,
    as if life on it depends;
      'tis naught I comprehend.

'Tis hopeful they'll arrive in good health,
    and nonetheless wealth,
Albeit be they in such a hurry—
    minds much all in such a flurry!

There were days in my childhood,
    'way out in the great wildwood,
It took all day on the wagon,
    hooves of mules slowly draggin',
To go into town and back
    by short-cuttin' 'crost
        the railroad track.

If we arrived in time,
    I'd spend my dime
On an ice cream cone
    and talk on the phone
To my city cousin—
    lotsa kid talk abuzzin'!

I'll follow the trail
    across the rail,
To hurry right back
    to my little shack—
Lest lost are my thoughts
    and strength of will
To settle down
    and pick up my quill.

Crescent on High

In half-blinded plight,
I thought 'twas just another light,
Hanging high o'er the city.
But oh, what a pity
Not to be more aware—
And to look with more care,
To discover a phenomenon—the crescent up there.
Whilst with beauty besmitten,
In awe, I'm stricken
With rate of speed this heavenly body has traversed,
As with quill and great effort, I have conversed!
What a glorious sight
To watch in the middle of night!
And 'twill vanish much too soon—
The waxing of the new moon!
(A treasurable boon.)
A crescent moon, sailing high,
Way up in the sky.
As it sails o'er mountaintops,
Peons like me, know not where it stops.
Now 'tis covered with dark clouds—
No more beauteous view allowed.

Crossroads of Life

Standing at the crossroads of life,
Watching the time whizz past,
It occurs to me at long last,
Strange ideas and decisions run rife.
I must hasten my pace to hurry,
Lest my thoughts should turn to worry
That time is swiftly passing by,
Sans more work that I should apply.
Let me cling to the tenets of life's creation—
Ne'er shall I waver to the trail of aberration.
I sit now to meditate
O'er long-lost dreams I no longer anticipate—
Albeit anon to merry song
As time marches on!
And multitudes of aged pass through tests of time,
None offering them solutions
To soothe their persecutions
As victims of time—
Naught life, sublime.

Crying Out at Night

I cry out through the night:
"Free me, O Lord, from the shackles of my plight.
In silence, I've experienced many years of strife,
And many sorrowful tragedies of life.

"Passionate, pent-up emotions are begging to be freed—
As has been decreed.
No longer can I abide
This imprisonment inside—
With pain—when there's nothing to gain.

"A sufficiency of literary desire
Can set the world on fire,
And break up sadness,
With the crash of a breakthrough
In literary madness."

Dawning of the Morning

The clouds were streaked with color,
Riding through on crests of light
Finding its way through vulnerable openings,
As daylight emerged from night.

'Tis the dawning
    of the morning
That brings inspiration most profound,
And awareness by the birds
    that bring such heavenly sound.

To live forever but ne'er to forget
Blessings in the country
That nature does beget.

For life in the city,
    thankful one must be,
But 'tis such a pity
    that nature here be little to see.

Days of the Best

The gleam of the beams
    shining up through the trees
As the sun sinks low in the west,
    and the cooling of the breeze
Brings days of the best,
    when better times were of no quest.
'Twas then our life was mostly perfection,
    and naught for else had we selection.
Happy were the ways
    of our yesterdays
When time stood still
    and thoughts were nil.

Dazzling Sunrise

I watched the dawning of the morning
From my perch upon the bed,
And the fiery ball of glory
O'er the treetops as it sped,
Bathing each cloud with changes of hue—
Perfect rapture, a new day to imbue.
And little feathered angels, flying from tree to tree,
So wondrously wild and free!
'Tis heartbreaking to see the beauty He has granted
So wasted in use, to be disadvantaged.
God grant us the privilege, Your endowments to use,
Plus embodiment of all blessings, profuse.
And empower us with the grace,
Glorious rapture to embrace.

Destiny

A writer I must be
    if it was meant for me.
A Higher Being said:
    "Take up your pen and write.
I'll instruct you day by day—
    and angels by the night.
Surely, by this time, you can see
    your destiny
        Is my decree.
So whate'er may transpire,
    your thoughts, do not retire.
Look on beauty and miracles I have wrought.
Miss not a single aspiration
    of nature's perfection you've sought.
Write down every literary treasure
    with which your mind is fraught.
You'll be glad you did, one day,
    when your burdens you lay down.
You've kept your covenant with the Master,
    and have won your crown!"

Diamond Trees

Brilliance of diamonds—with facets, galore,
Sparkling through trees, by the score—
    Bedazzled am I
     As I go on a "high"—
Just sitting here watching the setting sun,
A sparkling spectrum, having just begun.

With this phenomenon each day I am blest.
Some say 'tis repetition at my behest,
But to this daily revelation, sublime,
There's never an end of time.

Doors of Reverie

Scopes of forest floors
Are openings to my doors
Of daytime reverie—dreams,
Portraying visualized scenes
      of fine-spun gold
        mine eyes to behold—
Closer scrutiny reveals
      mounds of straw
        from the pine above,
Laid by nature's caring love.

Dream Castles

Flecks of radiant sunlight are dappled on the trunk
Of a half-dead oak—just a rotten old chunk—
What's left of my tree house, standing there, outside,
Where mostly, as a kid, in there I would reside.
Take me back, O drifts of time,
To innocent thoughts, once so sublime,
With unclogged reveries so sweet,
And cool breezes on little feet
Propped up high against the wall
Of my little hut, under trees so tall.
There I dreamt away my days,
And concentration was a haze.
Childish thoughts were unencumbered;
Dream castles arose, by the number!

Dream World Kingdom

I'm in a dream world of my own,
Sitting all alone on the gilded throne
Of autumn leaves and dried grass,
Sans exposure to crowds en masse.

Here I go, confusion to escape,
And around my kingdom to perambulate,
With beauty of nature from sky to ground,
And wondrous scenery all around.

Come with me to my little lair,
Where joyous contentment, without a care,
Is ever present as a summer breeze,
Where birds are singing in all the trees.

Each Day, Thankful Be

Each day is a new revelation to me,
Of just how wonderful life can be—
The glory of the sun, the wind, and a tree,
Are sufficient manifestations for me.

Dazzling colors of the spectrum
Leave me spellbound on my lectern,
Blinding my scope of view,
Precluding my every clue

As to Sol's route at the end of each day.
Through the twinkle of leaves, try as I may,
I lose trace of his escape,
And further efforts are futile to make.

To have lived just one day,
To hear old songs of yesterday,
Is more than sufficient reason
     to thank God for this one more day.

Early Morning Blessings

Comes a gleam
    o'er the scene
        of illuminated pines.
Such perfection Rembrandt would covet,
        in all of its designs.

He could not want for splendor
        more appropriate than this—
His work suffused with grandeur
        would be such perfect bliss!

Take not from me the beauty
        of my little rustic glen,
For 'twas there that I have written
        of things way back when—
Give to me the blessings of the early morning sun,
And the glorious spectrum colors
        when end of day has come.

Early Morning Thoughts

In the early morning darkness
    come helpless shadows of thought—
Aftermath of mistakes from experiences wrought from
    naught.
Could I but recall opportunities that were mine,
Methinks perhaps 'twould fall,
    everything much more in line.
And in the early morning hours
    (which time for me is best)
I could then take my rest—
    Not to spin, toss and turn,
While in mind my bridges burn.
With sleepless hours tossed away,
    I bid good morning to another day!

Earth Angel

A beam of sun is shining
Through my little house of play.
For mem'ries I am pining,
More than I can say.

Many are the moments
    have I sat throughout the day,
Dreaming of how when I'm grown up
    I would slip away,
Into the outside world
    of fascinating things,
And those exciting adventures
    that later life can bring.

And before the day is ended
In my Playhouse Shang-ri-la,
Tranquility has descended
And my thoughts have all blended.

I've tried to find a model
    I could pick for my role,
But none have seemed to be
    a match for my soul.
So I've elected to become
    an "Angel on Earth"—
Perhaps 'twas so my destiny,
    same day as was my birth.

Efforts and Burdens

A small green jungle surrounding a light green trailer
In a cove at the end of a hill
Is where I go to write poetry and listen to the trill
    of the cute little wrens on the window sill—
And where, in silence, I meditate
    and pray God to indicate
What changes in life I should make,
For my efforts, my burdens shall soon o'ertake,
Upon which time, my perseverance I shall forsake.
God grant me the grace and the strength to pray
That on the path of struggle I shall stay.

Embers of the Past

Albeit I a poet be,
Naught, no more, as such is he—
Not a kindred thought with me,
Be it not as it may,
That thoughts of now or yesterday
Are naught but thoughts all washed away.
'Tis not a case of Barrett
     nor of Browning, either one,
But now as ever, come what may come.
Up the path of blind contrition,
Tread we now, in admonition
Of the past, so long ago—
Memory of which we can't let go.

Evening Peace

Evening sun shafts crost the meadow,
Gleaming beams on the forest floor
'Neath canopies of trees,
    growing there by the score.
Awesomely mystic, come many emotions,
Borne on wings of tranquil serenity,
Swept on and on, in waves of solemnity,
Further and further, along the way,
As comes ending of the day—
Now sweet and low, sound tranquilizing notes
    of peace and love,
        from birds' sweet throats.

Evening Prayer

The sun, through the trees, is shining bright.
On late summer roses,
Each bloom reposes,
As approaches the night.

Soon hushed are the voices of birds so sweet
As to their nestling ones they chirp, "Tweet, tweet!"
Reverberating through the trees,
His Highness do they please.

Hark! The stillness in the woods.
For peace of mind, it is good.
Oh, my reverie do not disturb.
Let not my thoughts now be curbed.

Lest I lose this fleeting light
Which 'round my head is shining bright.
Pray, Lord, do give me some endurance
To gain thy favor and assurance.

Extant Celestial Glory

Little specks of heaven
    flung from the Master's hand,
Seemingly, with ease, as if the flurry
    of twinkling stars
Had come from distances of far less span—
Dimensions of strength (of weakness, naught),
Ethereal beauty and love had brought
From extant celestial glory,
With no less than perfection
    in telling the story.

Extension of Time

Be not saddened that I leave thee,
Most bountiful nature, divine.
N'er more hath treasured blessings
Been endowed so much as thine!
Grandeur of the heavens,
      in colors so sublime,
With awe, fill me with wonder,
      as I realize they're all mine.
In this sense of appreciation,
I am gripped with consternation,
Lest I leave before I'm sated
With the treasures bestowed upon me
Through omnipotence of Thee!
Would not I'm so ill-fated!

Eyes of Stars

She stole the stars from the skies
To make the gleam in her eyes.
As he kissed her gifted hands,
He was a slave to her commands.

Little did he know
    that she'd one day, cease to glow.
Albeit, for life, loyalty he vowed,
The day did come when he never bowed
As she passed by,
    not heeding the glance
      of his anxious eye.

There'd come a day when he would see
Miss Right for him,
    with never more to be
    a feudal slave decree!

Fascinating Creatures

The sunbeams shine
    neath the towering pine
To warm the nest of the twittering little things,
Giving strength to their trembling little wings.
Here comes Mother Wren, a buggy in her beak—
She stuffs it into the nearest mouth
    with a gentle little tweak.
Then here comes Daddy Wren—
    for the second mouth, a worm,
Alternating, on and on,
    till each has had his turn.
I've never been more fascinated
    with any creature God created,
And, if left to me,
    for me to see,
        verily, 'twould be
Life forever,
    indefinitely!

Fiery Imagination

Tons of fiery sunshine tumbled onto the roof.
What more need we of proof
That around us there's such glory?
To exemplify the story:
      In one great booming crash,
      creating a state of awareness
      in a vivid flaming flash—
      myriad waves of sensation!
      With metaphors of inspiration!
      Most awesome in all creation!
In breathless realization, most profound,
Come we back down,
To earth's firm ground!

"Flame of Life"

The mocking bird kept singing in the twilight,
While a fiddle was sawing out "Over the Waves."
With thoughts not bright,
Crying out in the night,
A heart in sadness, craves
One more chance, the flame of life to ignite.

To stop the moon from shining,
And make the winds lie still
Is naught more impossibility
Than love of life reach nil.

'Tis so the hands of justice
Creep out and o'er the hills—
And, slowly, on and on,
The gods turn the mills.

Flecks of Reflection

For one fleeting instance
    a spot of light shone
On a pole of the phone,
    protruding above my home.
'Twas such a tiny reflection—
    mystically a connection
Between substance and light
    which, by the next moment,
        had taken flight.
But resolving the relation
    of all things in creation,
'Tis a bit of food for thought,
And to say I know, 'tis naught;
Where does it go from here—
That bit of light that was so near?

Freddy, My Angel

Wake, for the night will soon be o'er—
Lest my dreams and fancies, having begun to soar,
Flee from my imaginings, and 'tis too late
To catch them before they pass through the gate
To my euphoric land of make-believe,
Where I must escape for my reprieve.
On this night, in particular, I am
      accompanying an angel
          through clouds that billow,
Like wispy white feathers all clinging to my pillow,
Supporting a laughing cherub, as gleefully he skis
Up through the billows, in an effort to tease,
O'er top of next cloud,
      and, merrily as he goes,
          singing out loud.
Now this dream was realistic
      and was very much so—
'Twas the infant that I lost
      so many years ago!

Friendship, a Treasure

If too immense are the spaces,
And too immeasurable, the places,
If fortitude begins to forsake us,
We mustn't let adversities o'ertake us.
'Tis faith and trust,
That garner, we must
If friendship, we treasure,
In every measure.

Fretful Clouds

Tossed in the breeze
Above towering trees,
Wispy bits of clouds
    go scurrying by—
Bits of feathery shreds
    clinging on, as if to cry,
Lest breaking off, they fall to earth,
To die before birth!

Come, little ones, do not fret—
Things of thirst, you soon can wet,
With your precious drops of rain,
From which much there is to gain!

From Whence, A Bard!

At dawn's first blush
    a radiant sun rises.
Above the tree tops, it's flush
With the top of the chimney,
Where billowy smoke abounds,
    enveloping the grounds
Of the old building standing
    there, so commanding,
On the path by the way
    where the schoolchildren play,
Reminiscent of the days gone by—
    My! How the time does fly!
Seems like only yesterday
    when as a child
        I used to play
On this same little old school yard,
From whence has come a bit of a bard—
Writes she, now, way into the night,
    by the faint glow
        of a small night light!
Hoping that soon she'll be apprised
    that at long last,
        she'll be recognized!

Friend Whippoorwill

I am blessed with the trill
Of my friend Whippoorwill.
He serenades me all night long,
With his fascinating song.
He's constantly in flight
Most all through the night,
In his quest for just the right place.
From tree to tree, he flies with grace
(with little concern for lack of space).
Sensing my need with nature to commune,
He follows me from room to room.
Up through the night air, above,
He soars, with merry notes of love,
His voice so divinely caressing—
What a really wonderful blessing!

Freaks of Nature

Little freaks of nature
    are beauties portrayed
    by a brush, mislaid,
When He stopped to shoot a star
O'er horizons standing afar.

It took a bit of planning
    to finish things on time—
Just about as long as to
    make a verse rhyme.

Faith

I shall thank God tonight when I pray
For the blessings I received today.
Then feelings of fear and dismay
Will be swept completely away.

As I silently ponder my plight,
No more is each day filled with fright—
For 'tis faith that will see me through
Sleepless nights, to begin day anew.

Genealogy of the Trees

'Tis a great hypnotic state
      from which I can relate
To the language of the trees
      as they circulate the breeze,

Exchanging wondrous stories
Of their myriad magnificent glories—
How they've evolved from trees of old,
With many ancient stories to be told.

Oh, how lucky the trees are—
They can gaze on every star,
And witness stellar phenomena in the sky—
More than any research can imply.

They can wrestle with strong winds
And hold their own what e'er descends.
Oh, sometimes they must acquiesce,
When their strength becomes sometheless.

And ofttimes 'tis so very good
That 'twill be well-understood.
Perhaps 'tis time to step aside,
Thus for younger trees to preside.

I'll hang my hammock from tree to tree
So that I'll be able to see,
And to watch in detail,
Every movement to entail

Transposition of the deposed,
Every step to be exposed.
In explanation, 'tis sensation—
The evolvement of creation

Of the forest in its realm,
As in splendor dost o'erwhelm.
'Tis thus I must take my leave
Till more manifestations I perceive.

Gentle Winds

Quietly, the morning breeze
    softly whistled through the trees.
With gentle ecstasy, the wind shifted
    to the downhill pull.
Scampering along before the next hill's lull—
    in-the-space
    ordinarily kept in its merry race,
It reached the top of the hill,
Careening round the corner with a musical trill,
And the warm sweet kiss of the wind's soft touch
Rustled crost the heap of colorful perfection
In nature's arrangement of her autumn collection.
Nearby the droopy willow, as she sleepily responded
    with lazy caresses
    of wispy tresses—
So soft, like down from the cottonwood tree on the hill
    o'er yon, beyond,
Just short of the sound of the boisterous whippoorwill—
Giving credence to supposition of things as planned
For interdependence of one to another,
To carry out instructions of One higher in command!

Glory of a Storm

Oh, the lightning was flashing,
And the distant thunder rolled.
Into trees it was crashing
As Ole Thor had grown so bold!
In my bed, I was covered, both head and ears,
Trying to drown my frightful fears
Of rumbling elements rent with spears—
Afraid, lest I know not when it clears!
Oh, the beauty of the flashes,
    when the sky with them is lit,
Brings to life a dormant glory—
    revelations, bit by bit,
Of His powerful omnipotence,
    shown with perfect grace,
All round the earth
    and outer space.

Glowing Tones

Across the east, glowed tone,
As light of all time
Minimized all things in her path as she shone.
She warmed the way as she traversed in pre-dawn routine,
Bringing life and warmth to the scene.
Now to be brightly alert,
Watching and waiting for glories, overt,
When at last appears a great red ball,
Accompanied by a medley of songbirds' early call.
'Tis the time of day that's best—
Until many hours later,
When comes splendor in the west!

Goals and Dilemmas

She looked up with eyes that were blind as could be,
And the one she was looking at, she could not see.
He was stricken by the yearning revealed in her face—
The embodiment of character, supported by grace.

Who knows in which field of accomplishment she could excel,
Had this accident of fate upon her not fell?
Many a precedent in life had she set
Before her antagonist ever she met.

All during school days, predictions were spoken,
That her vows to reach goals would not be broken.
Never spoken were words other than compliment,
By instructors of classes in which time she had spent.

God had a plan of a different direction,
For a pattern of fate that would make a connection,
Despite the loss of her power of speech,
And albeit a stalemate she would reach.

God gave her talent to dance and sing,
And soar to heights like a bird on the wing,
With expressions of manifestations of nature,
And His own love, in His powerful stature.

Bringing to life, things otherwise dead,
Survival of which had hung by a thread,
Revealing a talent so very rare,
With which nothing else could compare.

Now she is faced with a different direction,
Choice of which seems not perfection.
God, give her guidance to help her along—
Pray not that her dilemma will be too long.

God's Gemstones

'Twas a hunk of uncut ruby, so extensive in size,
Oh, what a prize!
Just blazing away!
Overwhelming were its rays!
It sparkled so bright
As it went out of sight
Down beyond the horizon.
I could hardly keep my eyes on
The most glorious of sunsets
That ever eyes would see—
Hiding behind a tree!

Golden Moments

Cycles of season
      o'er the changing years,
Have naught for much to reason
      nor anything to fear.

Softly sighs the willow
      beside the old grist mill.
O'erhead the white clouds billow,
Soon to wash the rocks and rills
Free of dust caused by the settlings
From the task the mill fulfills.

Now, in my second childhood,
I reminisce the moments, dear—
How I used to wade and splash
In the millstream, cold and clear.

New ideas are wont to pervade,
As pleasant thoughts begin to fade—
Memories from ages, old,
      must I enshroud
          in moments, gold.

Gone Are the Simple Days

Let me look and enjoy
Life's fulfillment me to buoy,
To inspire me with life
Amid toil and strife.

As I look through the trees
And feel the cool breeze,
In these May pre-summer days,
I wonder: How come such a maze?

Making my way about town,
Crowds all run me down—
Inconsiderately, not using courtesies of traffic,
Not giving a hoot about their own lack of it.

Take me back once more,
To yon distant shore,
Where life was simplicity,
With nature's own complicity.

Grandmother's Advice

Throw discretions to the winds;
You can later make amends.
Matters not what they may say—
This does not happen every day.
So when your charming prince comes by,
Give him that "come hither eye,"
And when he starts to come your way,
Think of something smart to say,
Like, "My, oh my! What a wonderful day!"
Surely that will catch his ear,
As he comes a bit more near.
Do not attract him close today;
Tomorrow is another day.
Do not flirt, and be not coy,
For he could be an experienced boy.
Fickle approaches may him repel;
So foolish sayings, do not tell.
Try to be both sweet and pure;
Without a doubt, 'twill him allure.
Take this advice (it always pays),
From good old great grandmother days!

Great Colors of Autumn

To absorb the russet beauty
    of the greatest colors of autumn—
    in elements of time I've caught 'em—
Their flashing brilliance in full hue,
In the next moment, gone from view,
Then displayed in elegance by the grand oak tree,
Outside my window where I can see,
On outstretched branches—just for me.
Even on a cloudy day,
The pin oak tree will whisk you away
To a fairyland of colors sublime,
Turning back pages of time,
    to the reality
    that "Poems are made by fools like me,
    but only God can make a tree."

Great Wonders

Massive bales of cumulus
    are suspended above the trees,
Wafting in different directions,
    in response to the kiss of a breeze,
Portraying artistic creations
    like brush strokes from a great artist's hand—
On the world's greatest canvas,
    reaching unlimited span.

'Tis hard to imagine such beauty
    can be the aftermath of a violent storm,
But man is not to question
    how great wonders are born.

Haiku

1. My, how time does fly—
Memories of days gone by—
Never to return.

2. Last rays of sunset
Gleaming through branches of the trees
Sets my heart at ease.

3. Dawns the bright morning,
After the breaking of day—
In the month of May.

4. Low hangs the black cloud,
Dark as the night—a white one
Goes scurrying by.

Halls of Wisdom

Albeit only dust,
      you could almost feel the crust—
Encapsulated with age—sublime
Were books from ancient sages of time—
In halls of wisdom and truth,
Ensconced in their categorized booth.
Methinks I heard from long ago,
Voices ringing in midair
      so very clear,
      yet, sweet and low,
Beckoning that I come.
'Twas as if anon
      opportunity would be no boon,
      as time would end too soon,
And no more would I be called
Lest I wait for times of auld.

Healing Manifestations

I've wandered far away from God,
And now I'm so all alone.
I've prayed for a messenger of hope
To show me the way to go home.

Yesterday at the peak of my misery,
When my spirits their lowest ebb reached,
I prayed to be given delivery
From pain, and then I beseeched

That an angel of mercy be sent me,
And my answer was meant to be,
For in walked a lady with a glow on her face,
And then everything seemed to fall into place.

She explained how I could be healed,
And miracles of God she revealed
From Bible verse of quotations,
And many other wonderful connotations.

My faith in humanity she restored—
A boost to inspiration, long ignored,
Rekindled my life forces,
Guiding me to different courses

For atonement and glory divine,
And many blessings sublime.
Thank God for manifestations
At His behest in all creations.

Heavenly Array

The sun was flashing joy
    across the great divide—
Of happiness and gladness,
    all one being could abide.
'Twas only just a heartbeat
    of time and distance away,
And an embodiment of spirit
    could bring color in full sway.

Magnificently resplendent,
    is the order of the day
As the heavens are arranged
    in an organized array.
But next moment, in an arc of brilliance,
    the rainbow has gone away!

Heavenly Creatures Up in a Tree

Rocking on the bough of the old oak tree
(Just as noisy as can be),
Is a nest of little birdies going, "Tweet,
    tweet, tweet."
Not much to see except big beaks
    and little feet.

Soon, for food, they'll be a-longing,
And in no time at all, they'll be a-songing.
What more's needed to make earth heavenly
Than a nest of little creatures up in a tree?

His Omnipresence

The skies were dressed with care—
Stellar positions were most rare,
When a spectacular phenomenon
     in the still of night
Lit up the elements
     with most illuminating light!

Lightning was flashing all around,
All the way from sky to the ground.

No mystery to me, it was—
The explanation is because
'Tis only the portrayal of His Omnipotence,
Bringing awesome glory of His ever Omnipresence!

Humble Wordage

Lay not aside my humble wordage,
Lest lost be knowledge of my bondage.
Wake me not, that dreams I've lost—
Oh, them, preserve, at any cost!

Buried are thoughts from eons ago,
Resurrected as ages flow,
Origins of which are yet unknown—
Besot misnomers standing so prone.

Being able to recall those precious ages,
With quotes of ancient, venerable sages,
Leaves me in a dreamworld, alone,
Albeit with memories, all my own.

Imprisonment in a Cocoon

Staring through gold of the curtains, worn
Stands the woman, so forlorn,
Hoping the birdie on a protruding limb
Will hop to the frays of a torn-out hem.

"Come, little one, and sing for me—
I'm a prisoner in here, you see.
Never an outside sound is there
Ever for me inside of here.

"I've lost the beauty of the outside world,
And in my cocoon, I stay curled,
Waiting and watching for my rescue,
And chance to bid these bars adieu.

"It hasn't always been like this.
My life in early years was bliss.
My thanks to Him for the glorious rapture
Encased in gleams I must recapture."

In Quest for Affection

Her eyes were dark wells of mystery—
Looking, seemingly in quest,
For explanation of her life history—
And for the reason she had been blessed.

With a soul-searing desire for affection;
Yet from an indefatigable collection
Of well-polished admirers
(Albeit not much as inspirers),

'Tis true, one must admit
That to herself none she would commit,
For none seemed to answer her needs,
As they all were lacking in deeds.

Though honorable they were,
In accomplishments they were bare,
And never, through her discriminations,
Could she arrive at delineations
Necessary to anticipate
A choice, in life, for a mate.

Joys of Yesteryears—Today's New Sorrows

Joys of yesteryears
      are today's new sorrows.
Ne'er, for one moment, add time
      that one borrows.
Hold fast to the belief
That in one moment of relief,
Time reverts to predestiny—
To erase a present calamity,
And set everything straight
Before it's too late.

Kaleidoscopic Glow

Through a break in the trees,
Comes refreshing breeze.
Bedazzled I am
As the sun just began
Descending low in the west—
'Tis the time I like best—
Blazing colors, every hue—
Such experiences are very few.
Whirling and glowing in kaleidoscopic view,
Each changing color is a phenomenon, new
To a novice who forever, with an open mind,
Is receptive to learning of every kind—
Even beauty in ugly, one can always find.

Last Thoughts of the Day

Long shadows are falling, anon beyond recalling,
Their length determined by the sun,
As twilight now will start to come.
Shrouded in silence, are last thoughts of the day.
Could but the tranquil peace now come back to stay.
Touched by the hand of fate,
Wherever providence may create
An element of being in times so rare,
Preparatory to culmination of loving care.
Many are people, potential friends to make,
With needed assistance offered, of which to partake.
Feeling bespangled and swathed in gossamer threads of
    joy,
No other thoughts shall I now employ.
I'm touched with tones of gloriana,
And sated with blessings of heavenly manna,
Hoping to pass through portals of glory,
And there, to tell the story
Of Jesus, Divine!
On through ages and pages of time!

Leaves Hanging On

Hang on up there,
      'tis for me to care,
And appreciate your beauty, rare.
But it, me, bereaves
That your gorgeous sister leaves
Have gone on before,
      falling to the floor
Of your own private park,
      where life is a lark,
With birds and squirrels,
      possums and owls,
And even some fowls,
Gracing your existence
      with their own persistence,
In living their nomadic style,
Making forest life better, meanwhile.

Life

There's no life at all
    till you hear a bird's call—
See the sun as it rises,
    as earth's burdens it disguises,
Its sparkling gleams in array,
    preparatory to one more day.
Watching squirrels forage for food
    is a blessing very good.
And watching cars whizz by
    is a reminder that I
Once drove at a furious speed.
'Tis so strange that now my need
    (for speed)
Has decreased at enormous rate—
Luckily,
    BEFORE IT'S TOO LATE!

Lifelong Quest

In my little haven of rest
Wherein fulfillment has been blest—
Here should end a lifelong quest
To find nature's beauty at its best.
In breathless awe, I stand in wonder,
A stricken state, me, to encumber,
As I stare out the window in disbelief
(I'm really awake, I discover to my relief),
One tiny branch of a tulip poplar tree
Waving variegated colors of gold and green at me!
Such a combination, I've never before seen—
A perfectly arranged pattern of an artistic scene.
In a crowded little space, but sequestered from the rest,
'Twas as if nature had started a beauty contest.
And this frail little tree, from where it stood,
Displayed far more beauty than other trees could.
I've staged my own private pageant for the trees,
And whom I have crowned, anyone sees—
Midst mounds of colored leaves—up to the knees,
Blessed with pleasure of heavenly cool breeze!

Life Force Enfolded

May heartbeats enfold
Vital life forces so bold,
When passionate flames are burning,
Ever for love in yearning,
Reaching innermost depths of a soul—
Heights of understanding, untold—
Until life on earth is done,
And everything's revealed in one—
One long last revelation
Of what's grasped from life's creation,
With hope and freedom of mind,
Faith and trust in mankind,
And perfection at its best—
From pits of desperation, lest
All that's good be washed away.
Anon, comes another day!

Like a Distant Star

Come shafts of sunlight, like a spotlight from afar,
From 'way o'er the hill, like a distant star,
Heralding the dawning of another day,
One which now is here to stay,

Till twelve hours later, from the opposite direction,
Comes end of this day of splendorous perfection,
Filling the sky with such wondrous hue,
Spectrums of color fill this awesome view.

Little Creatures

Nothing is so tranquil as a cricket's chirp.
His little world, please do not usurp.
In the density of the deep,
Many tiny creatures sleep—
Away from mankind do they keep,
Lest the footprints of the huge
Take them down in a deluge
Of muddy waste and watery drain,
From whence they'll ne'er emerge again.

Lost in the Wilderness

What should have been best days of life,
For me, turned into toil and strife.
Gone are my carefree plans for peace,
And my days of pleasure, when I'd release
Myself to a much less rapid pace,
Allowing me to grow old with charm and grace.
The way I chose reached not my goal,
Nor pleasant amenities, unnamed—manifold.
I'm lost in a wilderness with no passersby,
And no one to hear my lonely cry.

Lost Soulmate

She's gone, completely,
    from the trail.
Efforts to find her
    are to no avail.
I've tried to erase her
    from my mind,
But absolution I cannot find—
My dear soulmate of long ago—
Memories of her, I cannot forego.
Albeit these thoughts I've verboten,
She is gone, but not forgotten.

(*Memories of my dear friend, Buren Douglas, member of the Bahai faith—Panama CZ, 1967–72*)

Love's Sweet Blessings

You're the flowers in springtime—
The autumn colors in fall.
The softness of your touch
    is wondrously sublime.
Your laughter is the tinkling sound
    beneath a waterfall.
The mother of my children,
    you were meant to be,
And all the other things
    that are dear to me.
God patterned you,
    and when He was through,
You were all the sweet things
    rolled up in one,
For me to love till life is done.
Thank God for blessings
    ever faithful and true—
But the one I thank Him most for
    is when He gave me you!

Love's Sweet Victory

She's a haunting melody
    from which he'll ne'er
    be free—
Just a heaven-sent bit of ecstasy,
As 'tis ever meant to be—
    Love's Sweet Victory!

Like a rose waiting for sunshine,
Her beauty enhanced by time,
So lovely to be gazed upon
    in breathless moments, sublime—
    a creation, so divine,
Like the wind's delicate kiss,
On the rose, in ethereal bliss,
Swept into realms of love's sweet song,
Where the sound of music is ever so strong.

Magnificent Manifestations

There's nothing so wonderful
    as the beautiful woods.
Through narrow escapes,
    I know why I lived—
To see and write as much as I could.

The tall, stately trees
    that the enemy would've cut
Are covered in color
    all the way to the ground,
    the most to astound—
There's nothing but color all around!

Thank you, Jesus, for letting me be,
Long enough living with ability to see
The magnificence of all these manifestations,
Through great omnipotence
    for all this creation!

Mama

Mama would have loved it out here in the woods,
Where everything is like, for what she always stood.
Tranquilized with silence as time stands still,
And loudest sound at night, the whippoorwill.
With tiny night-creature sounds pervading the breeze,
And warm winds softly rustling leaves
     in the trees.
'Tis all Mama could have wished for,
     to have been so pleased.

Meditations

The dark and the deep of the woods by the way
Are so pleasant to look in all the long day.
Cooling and restful, sounds like the trickle of the stream
As it winds its way through the center of the scene.

I could sit here forever, as time stands still,
While I listen to the whir of my little flutter mill,
Hoping for a glimpse of the heron at the brink
Of the stream where he often comes for a drink.

I hope I can come back here one of these days,
Having been around the world (it seems always).
I'll build a little tree house and do my meditation,
And hope for no end to this wonderful creation!

Now when I get back to my little retreat,
At the thoughts of which my heart skips a beat,
No one can take these memories of mine . . .
These precious minutes, oh, so divine!

Every cleansing thought of moments, sublime,
Will inner sanctums of my soul, refine.
O, God, pray not my thoughts to sever;
Please, do let them last forever!

Memories of Old

Leave me not go back
    to terms of practicality
While I feel my soul dancing,
    beyond realms of reality,
Past stages of anguish
    I'd heretofore borne—
Pangs of terror, I'd've now shorn.

From the brink of a chasm
    on which I sit,
Away goes sanity
    in one quick flit!
Come back to me,
    mem'ries of old,
That I, your treasures,
    may enfold.

Metaphoric Sounds

'Tis such a joy to me—
The metaphors I set free.
May they reach across the sea,
to sail upon the wind.
From me, they will transcend—
voices not to be denied,
Gently echoed by the tide.
At times methinks 'tis heard,
Tinkling notes of a musical word
Like a chorus of ethereal sounds—
Perhaps guardian angels making their rounds.
Or dolphin friends, it could be,
      sent from the sea
to check on me!
May their divine voices to me be lent,
Apprising me that they are heaven-sent!

Miracles of Nature

Clusters of russet on a green background,
Window frame pictures on which to expound—
This time of year, as the cycle comes 'round,
Overwhelming color combinations abound.

Hurry to sit; let imagination flit.
Make haste to capture every little bit
Of wonderful color while it lasts—
Alas! 'Tis sad it goes so fast—

Here today and gone tomorrow,
While ne'er more time can it borrow
To grace the land on which we stand.
It's back to nature, recycled by demand.

Miss Sensation of the Waves

'Twas the mighty roar of ebbtide
As emptied were the sands of the ocean side,
Into the chasms where sea creatures sleep
(Unaware of existing in a bottomless deep),
Or that there's another world up there,
Or that that's the place of existence where
The lovely sea maiden longs to dwell,
And such lingering quests she cannot quell.

She fights her way through the whooshing waves,
And the farther she goes, the more she craves
To see the place where landlubbers go
Before she returns down below.

On the verge of her emerging
Comes the powerful tide, surging,
In mountainous waves, obscuring all creation.
And on top of the waves, sat Miss Sensation,
Arms outstretched with loving care,
With the world, her beauty to share!

Molly

There was a little dolly named Molly.
Mommie took her one day on the trolley.
So in love with the crowd was she wont to be,
She begged that she could be able to see
Above all the heads of the passersby,
Until other dollies she did spy.
"Oh, Mommie, can I stay?
And here I can play
With these dear little folks like me.
Oh, once, do answer my plea!"

So worried was Mommie that Molly she might lose,
She begged this time her baby to excuse
Her from granting her wish—
Rather, come see her dish

Of candies and cookies made by Mommie's own hands—
The most that ever could meet her demands.
There were all sorts of goodies decorated with holly,
And pacifiers of lollies, by golly!

Now Molly did eat of all the good treats
Till her eyelids became heavy with sleep.
All wrapped in her 'lectric blanket she slumbered so
    deep
        that
She dreamt of a boy doll named Wally—
And a pretty green parrot named Polly.

Now list to this fable
    and if you are able
        to figure it all out,
Do call me up soon and tell me about
How all this did begin.
This story, do not rescind—
For this wonderful bit of sweet inspiration
Does give Mommie great elation.

In her wonderful imaginative mind,
All at once did Mommie find
That now without family or either a spouse,
She's just a little girl playing house!

(*Written 12-24-93, on Molly's seventy-first birthday!*)

Moonrise

To hail its ascent
And blessings to present
With its entrance on the scene,
Sending out its wondrous beams—
This glorious sliver of a moon,
Waxing toward a fullness,
Coming, to be soon!
It graces the sky
As it races by,
Having many more passages
With which to comply.
But oh, what a blessing
When me, it's caressing
With soft rays from faint light,
As it goes out of sight,
From across my window sill,
Other appointments, to fulfill.

Moonset

There were shafts of moonlight, bright—
'Twas naught but sheer delight,
As it gleamed across the night.

The moon was setting,
    with no time for letting
Thoughts flee from an active mind,
Ideas ne'er more to find.

In blissfully stricken silence,
I watched the daylight overtake the moon!
In the blink of an eye,
    the phenomenon of the setting,
        alas! Was gone too soon,
O'er the hill—
    my heart, with awe, to fill!

An aftermath of light
    glowed long into the night—
This night sky of splendor
    is one to remember!

Moonship

A lopsided moon hung overhead,
As I looked from my bed,
Straight through the window,
    to see of it as much
      as possible
    (through treetops and such),
On its course as an imaginary ship,
    sailing across the sea—
'Twas ever so realistic to me,
    as if 'twere really meant to be
      a galleon on a stormy sea—
And the sailors (in midair)
    cried out in despair,
      "Don't give up the ship!"

Hanging up there,
    suspended in the air,
Half-balanced on a treetop, high,
    topsy-turvy and running awry
      as soon as the sea ran dry.
I watched it go down
    (still not so round)
Through treetops
    that to it had extended
      support
        until its journey ended.

Most Beautiful Time of the Year

Ah, the beauteous bounty of leaves outside!
One's housebound condition is much to be decried.
The most beautiful time of the year—
When winter is coming near.
In every direction,
There's nature's perfection—
Puts Monet and Rembrandt to shame!
As fall, its colors, acclaim.

Mural of All Murals

If an artist I could be
And also blest to see
How to capture on canvas
Feelings whirling around inside me—
To observe a wondrous sunset,
With the whole world aglow!
Could I but live forever,
A repetition of all this splendor,
'Tis for sure I'd never know.
In every direction,
A heavenly view of color perfection
From the west
In blends of the best,
Following relinquishment of the powerful sun,
After-effects began to come.
From brushes of the Master of all arts,
Comes the mural of all murals,
To capture the heart—
A mushroom-effect of gold and gray—
'Twould carry all spirited emotions away—
Mystic reflections, unsurpassed in color,
Shone the whole world around,
All the way to the ground!
A phenomenon most profound!

Musical Serenity

There was a calming tranquility all around,
Coming from mystic, Celtic lands—there to be found,
Softly sophisticated classics,
      enhanced by nature's sounds,
hauntingly beautiful music
      of deepest reverence,
Warming melodic meditations
      of gentle folk, with benevolence—
A music that inspires your dreams
      and softens your days,
With a serenity that relaxes
      the inner spirit, always!

My Creature Kingdom

How I love God's little creatures.
Each and every one He features,
Except, of course, an old mean snake,
Which I shall kill with my rake.

A precious little green frog,
Around behind a log,
Comes hopping down the lane,
Hoping for some rain.

And the lizard in the grass
Goes whizzing right on past,
Chasing a big brown bug—
My! He looks so smug!

Matters not which way I look,
I can recall shots I took
With that old camera in the closet—
S'pose by now I've probably lost it.

Getting back to the finer things of life—
The feathered kingdom, with no strife.
They all support one another,
In nature, one way or the other.

The tiny wren scratches like a hen,
Looking for crumbs while the jay moves in
To look for bigger pieces of food—
Some the dogs left, which are still good.
Now there's no fight with little Miss Wren
She'll go away and come back again.

My Friends, the Wrens

Little wrens, at their best,
Are building for themselves a nest,
To raise their family,
In a niche on a tree.
Through my window I can view
Busy developments as they pursue
Their building, in each stage,
Each step, as they engage
In preparation for their home,
Where they can be left all alone,
To perpetuate nature's game,
Whereupon they may proclaim
The birth of a nest full of
      precious little friends—
A wonderful cacophony of baby wrens.

My Mark in Music

Throughout life, I've tried so hard
    to leave my mark in music.

And with prayerful supplication,
    I'll watch till He reviews it.

My Peace

Give me peace and tranquility,
That in privacy I may be found,
Where I can think and use my ability
To write down thoughts, profound—
Where I can listen to the voice of silence
(One can learn so much that way),
Thence to be stored in the bank of memory,
To resurrect and use another day.

My Prayer

With manifestations from realms of glory,
Blessed is the one who tells the story
Of the cross He died on, hanging there,
To show his people He did care;
To rescue them from the mire,
And save their souls from hell fire.
Thank You, Jesus, for showing the way.
To follow Thee (if I may),
Is my goal in this life,
Midst the toil and the strife.
Though my cross is heavy to bear,
The lighter it is because You care.
Heaven's gates please open wide
As I lay my burdens by the river side.
I'll cross over and come inside,
Where I shall worship at your feet,
And absorb your nearness, oh, so sweet!
My heart is opened now, dear One,
And I pray that in, You will come,
To cleanse and save me from my sin,
And please erase where I have been,
Where waves of evil, all roughshod,
Over me, have ever trod.
My thanks if You will consider me
Consecrated, Lord, to Thee.
And as I lay me down to sleep,
I pray, dear Lord, that You will keep
Me safe from harm
And my heart warm

With care and consideration
For others with appreciation,
Who could help to pave my way
For peace and love on another day.

My River

The river of no return,
Sometimes wild and free,
For me, ne'er shall be
Back from whence it comes.

In my little canoe,
'Tis ever, as in lieu
Of technology and planes of height,
Forever I'm tied to dreams in my plight.

Since happenings have ever been,
I shall always remember when
My thoughts followed the flow
Of wherever the river might go.

My Sands of Time

My sands of time
Are slowly drifting away
In a whispering rhyme,
Begging not to stay.
And vibrations of peace are gently calling
From afar, as the night is softly falling,
While all around manifestations of nature abound.
Come back, come back, little grains of sand.
Shouldn't time stand still (until)
What I've planned
    is ready to fulfill?
So many are the poems that I have written—
The awe of the sunset by which I'm smitten,
And strata of rainbow colorful hues—
To do justice with a brush
    would only light a fuse,
Bringing to mind a spectacular celebration,
Such as seldom is seen
    for a birthday of our nation.

Nature's Diamonds

A million sparkling diamonds
    hanging in the trees,
Uninterrupted by the breeze—
    Treasures untold,
      They sparkle like gold.
Awesome are they to behold,
Values of which are unforetold—
    Bedazzling one minute,
    The next is the limit
To my daily view of the sun,
As it sets when day is done.

Nature's Free Beauty

One of the greatest things in life
Is that nature's beauty is free.
Spectrum of colors in the trees,
Nature patterned as meant to be—
A heavenly mixture of evergreen and gold,
Prettier than ever could've been foretold.
Senses being so very keen,
Such kaleidoscopic suffusion of color and light
Never before was seen!
With a cacophony of bird notes, come what may,
'Tis no wonder they stay in the trees all day.
Nature's wondrous beauty
    with which I'm not sated,
Is the magnificence of splendor
    so celestially fated—
From beginning of creation,
    the ethereal spirit
        of life's sensation!

Nature's Gems

Let not the sun stop shining
    on the greenery o'er the hill—
Thereto my eyes can feast
    until they've had their fill!
The sunbeams keep a-bouncin'
    off the dewdrops on the leaves.
'Tis the most of genuine diamonds
    that anybody sees.
I'll sit here on my stool by the window
    in the hall,
So as the sun is changing angles,
    I can see it all!
I grieve to say adieu
    to my little drops of dew,
As Ol' Sol is climbing upward
    to where'er he's hastening to.
I'll be here on the morrow
    when at first it's broad daylight—
And the great consuming rays of heat
    have chased away the cool of night.
I'll be richer than the richest
    as, busily, I count my gems,
And miserly as the miser,
    with treasures that no one spends.
I'll wait here on each morning,
    just as the day is dawning—
Sated by the beauty of dew diamonds in the sun—
Blessings to be honored till my last day is done.

Nature's Life

Oh, the gold and silver twinkle
    of early sun upon the leaves!
To the heart it is a medicine,
    and the eyes, the more to please!
The bumble bees are hummin'
    and little Woody is a-thrummin'
Across the bark of an old dead tree,
Where he's building himself a home,
And he can look out and see
If Mrs. Woody is coming yet,
To see the dwelling that's a sublet
From Mr. Nature of the Woods,
With whom in good stead they've stood.

With hopes and good wishin',
Perhaps we'd go fishin'
To the creek at the foot of the hill—
A cool stream rippling, o'er rocks and rills,
Just gurgling the time away—
No cares or worries, all the live-long day!

'Tis here one comes, leaving behind all strife,
To take a vacation and get a new life!

Nick (NK)
(Author's husband, now deceased)

On his little utility wagon,
    sits a dear old man outside.
He has everything in life
    that loneliness can provide.
His back and hands are bent with age—
At performing bits of miracles,
    he is a unique sage!
As an eccentric recluse, of the world,
    he's afraid
That possibly his privacy,
    they might upbraid.
Of this universe, he's seen all that to him appeals,
And has no further desire, his knowledge to reveal.
It takes quite a while to gain his trust—
To attain his presence, patience is a must!
Should you ever become his audience,
    fountains of knowledge to you is he,
And for hours he volunteers
    stores of treasures, all for free!
As his chosen aide and keeper,
There's no time to be a sleeper.
An unsolved mystery 'twill ever be,
And only God can so decree
How his energy is supplied,
As every moment he's occupied!

Night Sounds

Night sounds!
    Most heavenly music
        in the world!
When nature's glories are all unfurled,
To tranquilize a dreamworld of sleep.
Those who with worries do weep
For the days gone by
    and for which they now cry.
Oh, but for the chance to recall
    opportunity to be free
        from a fall
To these limitless chasms of sorrow,
And to listen to the night sounds
    and look forward to tomorrow.

November '99

This first day of November
Is nothing like September!
'Tis dark, humid, warm and depressing—
No wispy clouds, treetops caressing.
And lack of spirit, so suppressing—
Attempts to cheer is loss of time,
Imagination, so supine—
No inclination toward the sublime.

'Tis naught for me, good vibrations,
Wave lengths nil for inspirations.
Autumn colors are all gone,
Each leaf drifting, so alone!
Leaving its mark where'er 'twill fall,
Its contribution: Enrichment of soil.
But comes Thanksgiving, with thanks to be,
For privilege of living in a land once free!

Oak Creek Canyon

The colors on the wall
of Oak Creek Canyon
Are not from the Banyan,
But the Aspen, so tall.
You may ask how
      they got to that height,
Unless a little birdie
      took a big bite
Of the seeds growing lower on a tree,
And then flew up higher—
      high as high can be.
(*Of reflections from life in Arizona*   1972–73)

One Yesterday

'Twas difficult to tell her age;
Like an animal in a cage,
She'd been placed, without thought or care—
Just left to deteriorate there.

All days throughout,
    she crept about,
Looking for something, no doubt—
Sorting and feeling,
    from floor to ceiling,

Searching for something lost
(Value of importance, not cost).
To paraphrase a title, I'd say:
She'd give more than "A Million Tomorrows
    for Just One Yesterday!"

On Wings of an Eagle

'Tis a blessing to be bonded as a child,
With little feathered beings of the wild.
A blessing that accrues,
And to then lose,
Is too much to be borne
By weakest humanity, so forlorn.
Albeit there are challenges of strife,
'Tis stewardship to be honored through life.
To be able to converse with a bird
Is better to have felt than heard.
To soar on the wings of an eagle,
Out yonder, unfettered by space,
Is the sweetest imagination to be given
By God, in all His Grace!
As one not of this world,
With all of earth's fetters unfurled,
'Tis better to be windward bound
Than to be shackled to the ground.

Passage of Time

Eons of time, in one fleeting moment,
Pass swiftly by
      in one blink of an eye.
Ere one thought be lost
      in considering the cost
To humanity, in multiples of time,
'Twould not now be naught,
Slowing wheels of time for thought—
(Solutions there which may be sought)
In a more suitable clime
Before the end of time.

Peace and Silence

There's peace to be had in each different field—
Peace on battlefields, by treaties, to wield
Peace in government and peace on the street—
Wherever there's a body another can greet.
But the greatest peace of all, to me,
Is the peace in tranquil silence!

Performance of the Trees

'Tis as if they are aware
That for hours I sit and stare
While they dance and roll,
With soft and silky, newly-budded leaves,
Performing as if for me they wish to please.
Like waves on the ocean, they billow
     in the breeze,
As fluffy, white clouds form a pillow
     for the trees.
Untouched by impurities,
     are trees where virgin forests grow—
And people, whose caring hands they know,
Are sorrowfully sad to see them go,
As heartless loggers cut them down,
     row by row!

Phenomena of Three

There was a phenomena, in a group of three,
A heavenly creation, just for me!
And they were all behind just one tree—
The moon, Venus and Mars, in perfect formation.
Only God could make such a miraculous creation.
Such an awesome trio is seldom ever seen,
E'en behind two trees, or betwixt and between.
'Twas not a visionary imagination,
But really an experience of sensation,
As satellite and planets peeked through the branches,
While the glitter of diamonds sparkled in avalanches!
A treasure for me, 'twill forever be!

Phenomenal Transitions

Wild and free, blow spirited winds
As full-flown spring transcends
    In all its glory,
      relating the story
Of the joy of things to come—
With compliments of the sun.

As to rollicking waves are the seas,
So to rolling tall tree tops
    is the playful breeze—
Like billowy rushing breakers
    with foam of mint green
Whipping waves to a crescendo
    in scenes, supreme!
I'll spend my spare moments watching
    the dance of the winds,
As the phenomenal transition
    turns winter into spring,
And Mother Nature, with her magic wand,
    gently wields and blends,
Arranging all the joy
    HER CHANGES CAN BRING.

Picturesque

Picturesque is an inadequate term
As applied to a lesson in beauty, I learn,
When viewing the untouched arrangement of nature.
Trees in their crowded growth and stature,
Leave nothing to imagination—
'Tis perfection in God's creation.
The aftermath of grandeur from rain on green leaves,
Emphasized by the sparkle that sunshine can bring,
Is more than the mind can perceive.

Playhouse Sites

There's a mini-forest
    with half-grown trees,
Far as one can see—
    a sight for eyes to please.
And looking all about,
    scattered, are playhouse
        sites, throughout!
Time was, when I was just a sprite,
Chances for me were very bright.

In my little inventive mind,
Many useful devices I could find,
To fit together for Dolly, a home,
In this wonderful place
Where we'd feel not alone!

Plea for Existence

Don't take me now, Jesus, for I'm yet not fit.
I've poems to be writ
      and need to think while I sit—
Dreaming up things I need to say
      before I call it a day.

Thank You, my Lord, for hearing my prayer.
      to know that You care
      makes life worthwhile
    And gives me courage to smile
      through my tears,
      and to allay my fears.

Poetry in a Sack

Her poetry in a sack,
    within a pack upon her back,
She hadn't far to go,
    but her feet were very slow.
Now time had passed her by,
    leaving her plans run awry.
So with haste, she must comply,
    lest her chances be lost, to apply
For publication of her work,
    to show the world she did not shirk
The talent her Lord had placed with her.
Now, with each step, she did concur
With well-laid plans that she must finish
Before her strength should so diminish,
Leaving beautiful thoughts tossed to the wind,
Scattered about, no ways to wend
    their way—or to capable hands, turn,
Begging help to fight those who would spurn
Long hours of labor diligently spent,
As efforts to bring blinded eyes closer,
    left aged back bent.
Stumbling along upon the road,
    heavier, by the minute, was her load—
None offering her a helping hand—
    by now so weak, she could barely stand!
Now what will become of the unselfish lady?
    In a selfish world where soon,
        just maybe
Great harm, to her, could occur
    and volumes of tears,
        her eyes did blur,
From realization that no one cares!

Precious Life

Life is so precious toward the end of time.
In every direction, splendor is divine—
Of nature's scenic beauty, to those memories I cling,
Magnifying in importance, small details of everything.
Many years ago I took not things for granted.
From one moment to next, awareness supplanted
Perhaps by things of naught import—
Not of worth to e'en report.
Small details I once ignored;
Them to review, for time I implore
Our great Creator's consideration
That I be granted some divination
Into the future, that I may look
Upon the plans of the great Book.

Predestination

In predestination had I not believed
Before (now that I have perceived),
And after which, blessings I've received—
The gifts of beauty that are mine
(Now and forever, the most sublime),
Convinced I am, thus, of this
(Notwithstanding a state of bliss),
That blessings are not happenstance,
Albeit, somewhat circumstance.
Thanks be to God for a life preplanned,
With every detail so well-programmed—
So much entailed,
       yet non-prevailed—
Due to perfection in coordination
And reception with appreciation.
The beauty I'm surrounded by
       is too much for my capacity
          to occupy.
So I'll ask permission, if I may,
To save some blessings for another day.
And hoping I am heaven bound,
Some beauty I'll take and spread it around!

Pre-Planned Existence

Wondering, was it this glassy sheen
That my Lord had foreseen
On outside beautiful leaves of a tree,
As my life was preordained, so many years ago.
At such early age He could decree,
As to how my life should go.

Now I a poet be,
        and that is how I see
Through ages of time
        and how things rhyme.

I'll take things as they are,
        perhaps through notes and bars,
Hoping messages to convey,
        in my own particular way.

And I hope 'twas in God's plan
For my arrival, and that I can
Leave my mark, albeit perhaps not immense,
But, I pray, of some consequence!

Queen of the Sky

A circlet of diamonds I did spy,
ascending up into the sky.
In explanation, I should imply:
A full moon enshrouded by branches of the trees,
Was doing its utmost, the eyes to please—
'Twas a diamond-studded tiara, befitting
a queen of heavenly affairs,
Who could climb each step so lightly—
all the way up the stairs.
With her wand, a touch of magic,
to each one as she passed by,
Was lighting up a stellar pathway,
as she strolled across the sky.

Quietly, Dawn Is Breaking

Quietly, breaks the dawn, o'er dogwood blossoms,
With the sentiment of spring being here—
Hastily squelching all need for yesteryears.
The ruling elements of a balanced life
Bring laughter, clarity, energy and love—
And peaceful tranquillity, like balm from above,
Bathing the world with beauty of creation,
Awaking mankind to sensation of realization,
Withdrawing from a privileged world,
To transcend to galaxies and distant stars,
Attainment of which, there are no bars.
Now awake all afresh, with a sigh,
As a dew-spangled day draws nigh!

Rainy Season in Dothan, Alabama

'Tis the rainy season in Dothan,
After a long, dry spell.
I thought it was only in the tropics
Where heat, the raindrops quell.
As soon as dark comes, quietly,
You can hear the raindrops, nightly—
Pitter-patter, on the rooftop;
Not, till morning, does it stop!
Oh, how my nightdreams attune
With the rhythm of the raindrops' tune!

Ratio and Proportion

As to the hound is the beagle,
So to a hawk, is the eagle,
As woman, so profound,
Is to man's coexistence,
And as notes in musical sound
Are complementing the lyrics.

Ratios could go on forever,
Unless God decides to sever
Those fouled-up pairs
of abomination
Who stir up his arrangements
Of perfect creation.

Ratio to Appreciation

To me, it seems to be
    that 'tis so plain to see
God elongates life equally
In ratio or proportion—
As to one's own emotions,
Guided by the amount of appreciation
For vastness of the wonders of creation.
After much circumspection,
(Being prone to reflection),
'Tis my way of thinking
    that sans stoic determination,
I'd long since have reached elimination.
But I'm still here today,
Thanks be to God and
    the Guardian Angels He sent my way.

Reclamation

My failure in justice
        to nature's beauty, I redress.
Exhaustion in words
        leaves nil my power to express
The extent of my appreciation
        of God's beauty, to impress
The ones of grandiose import,
Who, from me, don't attempt to extort
My very life's blood,
        given in efforts to attain
Justification that existence for me
        has not been in vain!

Rhapsodic Musing

In a rhapsodic state of mind,
    musing, while trying herself to find,
She sat viewing the windswept trees,
    from which whirling, cascading leaves
Came endlessly sailing by—
    tiny sailboats floating from the sky.

'Twas a sunny autumn day
    and the squirrels were all at play,
Celebrating a rich harvest for the fall—
    so acrobatic, were they all!

The birds were singing merrily,
    for close to leaving, they were happy to be
On their way to a warmer land
    to continue their existence as so planned.
Next spring will bring the rain
    and return of the birds,
To start life's cycle
      all over again!

Rhapsody

A rhapsody is the love of heaven,
The bread of life,
      in which days to leaven,
Betwixt days of departure
      and re-entrance.
'Twill not be happenstance,
      nay, nor for instance.

A millennium for atonement and correction
Is to be had before the great election—
For testing wings
      for the flight of infinity,
In that realm of choices
      in divinity.

And those of the good
      have not to ponder,
But those of evil have many days
      in which to wander!

Rhymes of Gold in Ages of Gray

There's a commingling of bushes by the old mill stream
Where, daily, I sat to evaluate dreams.
Some were unusual, but to my satisfaction,
    naught had gone to the extreme.
On such an occasion
    I was approached by an evasion
Of temptations to change my direction,
Which immediately resulted in dissection
Of beautiful things
    created by dreams.
'Twas then that life went awry;
    nothing seemed to comply
With conditions that were pleasant—
    from past, nor in present.
Now in Ages of Gray,
    I drifted away
From things that led me astray—
Back to thoughts of old,
    to myriad Rhymes of Gold!
'Tis there that I hope to stay
    till Jesus takes me away!

Rhymes in Dreams

Rhymes in a sleepy dream
Are the ones that are most supreme—
Far superior in elements of dreamy bowers,
To those of daylight hours.

Dreamy persistence
      in nighttime existence,
Bordering on wakeful insight
Into minds of artistic awareness

Of time, which, when in flight,
In a certain state of being,
is wont to find
Once in life, peace of mind.

Rose of My Heart

A rarity beyond description—a treasure
    without measure,
The budding rose of my heart,
    with which ne'er could I part;
A rose of many colors, as the light passes through—
Each shade as it emerges, is something all brand new.
As I glance out through my window,
    with awesomeness I'm struck.
O'erwhelmed by such beauty,
    I've not the heart to pluck.
So, to each one of my friends,
    description must suffice.
Protection for this perfect rose,
I'll supply at any price.

Rustic Scenes of Nature

A rustic scene
      I am able to glean—
A kaleidoscopic array,
      on my nature walk of the day.

Bees are a-hummin' 'round the apple trees,
Pollinating each bloom, as nature decrees—
Preparing for the honey they'll make for the queen,
Whose royal taste is very keen.

Dancing shadows on the sweetgum leaves
Are swaying in the breeze,
As free as they please,
Hoping not for surcease.

The birds of season
      are celebrating (for no reason),
Singing their song
      all the day long.

So it seems to me
      that happy, one should be
That God created birth
      and this spectacular earth!

Sacred Vows

She danced by the light of the moon,
Dreaming of vows,
      with her warrior, she'd take soon.
As she floated in the brook,
      midst her flowing raven tresses,
She could imagine her lover's tender caresses.

Cleanliness is Godliness, and
      for her husband, she'd prepare,
With purity and sanctity
      of the union they'd soon share.
To the beautiful Indian maiden,
      future life's a sacred boon,
As she dances by the light of the moon!

Sans Freedom

Exponentially, with force, spake they—
What wont were they then to say?
"Fellow countrymen, what life have we
If we are not allowed to be free?
Draw your pistol, lift your sword—
Those streams of adversity we shall ford.
Our bridges, behind us, we'll not burn,
And, alas, 'twill be some naught return."

And so it's been since beginning of time;
War and peace must we entwine.
Hardly ever has peace there been—
Just bloody wars, to compound sin!
No one knows just when He'll come—
Like Aurora Borealis, brighter than sun.

We shall fall down on our knees;
'Twill be too bright for us to see.
This is what I've been told—
'Tis handed down from sages, old!

Second Childhood

Bright shines the light through the mini-blind.
To me, this experience is one of a kind,
And lends to the state of my peace of mind—

Taking me back to days of childhood,
And my escape in the wildwood.
For hours, watching birds, there I stood.

To me now 'tis clear,
And is well-understood,
What is meant when I hear
About a second childhood.

Save the Trees

As I roam o'er hills
    through rocks and rills,
        my greatest thrill
Is watching the trees go wild,
Their mighty strength profiled—
Dancing and swaying in expectation
    of an approaching storm
(For so long they have stood forlorn),
Hoping for an end to the drouth,
Roots branching out, almost to the mouth
Of the vanishing streams,
    once free-flowing springs—
Now thirsting for moisture
    and relief that rain brings.
Oh, Mr. Rainmaker, come pray with me!
    Let's save our wonderful trees!

Scorn of a Storm

I'm watching a storm
    evoking its scorn—
It seems to be quite a bender.
Dense trees in the forest are tall,
    with tops yet tender.
There's endless fury embosomed
    by the winds—
With Omnipotent strength,
    the trees, He bends.
The wind, in its force,
    can strangle the growth
        of a tree so tender and young,
With their boughs not yet well hung.
But God, in His wisdom,
    gives survival to the fittest
Among the sacred givers of life,
And to the people who toil in strife.

Sensational Vibrations

The world's alive with sensation,
'Tis the greatest day of vibrations,
Conglomerations of colors, galore—
Of beauty, there'll never be more.

I've exhausted my vocabulary
('Tis no longer a word constabulary),
Trying to describe
All the beauty outside.

To think how I became
So enthusiastic, in vain.
To me it has occurred
There's no way with simple words.

Alas, with time to think,
I'm all out of sync,
Attempting to portray color with pen and ink—
Not even the most elegant words could approach the
    brink.

So just look with your eyes;
There'll be no color disguise.
'Tis pure beauty that you'll see,
And 'twas meant for you and me!

I'll try now to restore the context
And get back onto the subject,
As to establishment of locations,
And an amount of great vibrations
(With an added dash of syncopation).

The reflections in the west,
While angles are at their best,
With the sun, bring out each color, true to test,
And the Lord sees fit to give at His behest!

Sensational Winds

A most spectacular view
      that my thoughts may imbue—
The passion of an approaching storm
Is conveyed to the trees,
      as if vibrations on winds are borne
To create an animation
      and set up a sensation
To be passed through the canopy all around
     through branches and trunks,
       on down to the ground.
One tree's inspiration is passed on around
Until the whole forest is twisting and rolling—
Once started, there's no controlling
The motion of tree tops' performance—
A glorious sight of nature's conformance!

Sequel to the Gypsy Violinist

Once was I into romance—
      'twas not for me, a happenstance.
Bells of passion tolled, so free—
My spirits, wild, reached across the sea.
And there my gypsy waited for me.
With wild abandon, our passion did burn,
The flame growing brighter at every turn!
For days and weeks, we played together,
Whate'er circumstances or the weather.
With low-moaning notes of my Indian Flute, I stayed,
To accompany the vibrato of violin he played,
Both day and night, in a haunting strain,
With heartfelt emotion—'twas almost pain!
This was all so very long ago—
      I now think back in saddened woe.
From across the ocean
    (on my ears, befallen),
His piteous wails to me are calling:
    "Come back, come back,
    my sweet, soul mate."
Oh, now, my dear, 'tis much too late.
Your spirit floats to yon distant shore,
      where we shall meet,
          to part no more!

She Sleeps in Peace

With every caw of a crow,
And every distant bark,
My imaginations flow,
And arouse a small spark
Of reality from when
Little capers she'd spin—
My Koni Wildflower,
In her peaceful little bower,
Where now she is resting
    with two sisters and a brother.
No more is she requesting
    supper in courses, one after another.
Sleep well, my darling baby—
    Soon you'll have your wings,
And join the happy chorus
    Where all the angels sing.

Silence of Morning

There's something in the silence of the morning—
Just before the dawning—
With the last few trills
Of the merry whippoorwills.

And the patter of little feet on my roof overhead,
Reminding me today that I cannot stay abed,
Lest the world outside may pass me by,
With nothing left on which to rely.

Sky of Splendor

God painted the sky with splendor—
A Rembrandt to remember.
The gold on blue
      and purple of the hue
Transcends all power of thought.
Efforts at description are but naught,
As I marvel at His magnificence
In portrayal of His omnipotence.

So in Love

Now you're gone,
    but my memory lingers on,
Echoing thoughts of, oh, so long ago—
So vivacious and coquettish,
    and so in love with you, was I—
'Tis true, when you were nigh,
Time was no more of the essence,
Rather, manifestation of quintessence!

Soulmates

Beams of hope flash through the air
    on my vibrations,
Searching for remnants of celebrations
From days gone past,
    when at long last,
A soulmate, I had found—
With thoughts so profound.

Mother, sister, and mentor, was she,
And all that a friend was meant to be.
Our religious encounters were very brief,
Albeit sufficient for pent-up relief.
But God saw fit, us to separate,
And now I will but wait
For her at heaven's gate!

(*Dedicated to Buren Douglas from days in Panama, 1967–72*)

Space

In all this world,
There's nothing so precious as space.
Denied this freedom,
She could only self-efface.
Humiliation and disgrace
She had borne with great distaste.
In a very few more months,
'Twould be the thirtieth year
Since began the loss of space, so dear—
At the time it was not so clear
That 'twould ever be so near
Imprisonment—like in a cocoon—
To become unbearable so very soon!
For more precious space,
there was ever-increasing need
And to constant arguments,
'Twould ever lead.
So antagonism and bitterness
Brought a health breakdown,
With ill-fated experiences to abound,
The most high-spirited people to astound,
In close-lying regions all around.
'Tis a very sad ending
To what could have been
Had not logical reasonings been so very thin,
And had more consideration been given
To everyday needs of one who's supposed to be
in charge of the mode of livin'!

Spectrums of Wonder

Overwhelmed am I with awe,
Seeing colors, all sans flaw.
Nature's paintings they portray,
In competition with Monet.

Of great imaginings to pursue,
I match spectrums with mind's view,
From an inner sense of timing,
For the right place to make a rhyming.

God's handiwork of unique perfection
Is shown in nature's annual collection.
Would that He give me the power of speech,
Descriptive justifications to reach.

In efforts to warrant His delegation,
Enabling me to show His creation
To a world so stricken with ennui
That they would cut down every tree!

God pity beings with no appreciation,
Who look upon beauty with no elation.
Thankful am I for ability to see
Wonders Thou hast created for me!

Stark and Staunch, the Trees

Naked trees are beautiful
    with their bare uplifted arms—
Dare they flaunt their unique charms
For all the world to see
How relentless they may be
In facing all adversity—
Vandalistic or heaven-sent,
    whate'er their destiny—
Stand they strong and proudly bent,
Away from whence the wind is sent—
Stark and staunch to each onslaught
To show now fear 'tis ever naught!
To quote Kilmer:
    "Poems are made by fools like me,
    but only God can make a tree."

Stringy Little Tree

It grows with a flair
    and when it reaches up there,
'Twill be the talk of village affairs.

But when given first to me,
    'Twas a stringy little tree—
Not worthy for people to see.

Through summer drouths it turned yellow
Albeit much water I gave the little fellow—
'Twas sufficient to carry it
    through ages, to mellow.

Then I started to visit my tree each day,
Hoping companionship and attention might pay
Dividends of happiness through spring
    and May.

I brought my musical instruments from inside.
I decided no longer, these I'd hide,
But would play them all with pride!

As I played, sweet and low,
Wilted leaves began to glow,
And I could see the tree start to grow!

All the birds joined in—
Heavenly voices to transcend.
What a wonderful feeling, coming from within!

Sunset and Twilight

Sunset in all its splendor,
Lit up a tree so tall and slender.
Overwhelmed was I (with sheer bliss)—
Such a phenomenon I never would miss.
I'm standing there all alone,
(After the sun is gone
O'er the horizon and down below),
Watching the lamp's low glow
Against the dark of the cloud—
With morbidity of night, the colors enshroud.

Sunset at Its Best

Only the Master can paint such a view—
Strata of color in every hue,
So brilliantly shining through trees in the west;
'Tis sunset at its very best.

With awe, I behold this phenomenon, rare,
Hoping to absorb each ray with care,
Knowing that for life this experience I'll preserve,
Albeit, however more I shall observe.

Sir Woody

Along comes Woody with a keen beak;
By this time, no one will speak
In self-defense, or otherwise—
For reasons one can well surmise.

So early each morning I do my bird watch,
Along same time as I do my coffee klatch.
What a way to start the day!
Not all work and not all play.
    (*Written on my eightieth birthday, May 4, 1996*)

Simultaneous Phenomena

The freshness of the morning
And the beauty of the scene
Were more than I could handle—
Phenomena, so serene.

Uniquely-arranged petals of a rose,
With magnificence of color to impose,
Casts much glory upon the world,
Blessings to humanity to be unfurled,

While sparkling and glistening
With diamonds of dew,
Proudly erected, reflecting the blue
Of the sky up above,
Motherly hovering, with love,

For tender little earthlings, below,
Trembling with appreciation, to show
How much more rarity we have in store—
Opening with mystic lore,

Embosoming this rose
On one of the lower branches.
Above, an opening bud
Sheds beauty in avalanches,
Promising a spectacular view—
Unexcelled, as none others could ever do!

Syncopated Rhythm

The syncopated rhythm of the
    twinkling of the leaves
Is heaven-sent to me
    as my vision perceives
The compatibility of nature
    through all the trees.
All day long cool shadows pervade
Through forests, bringing shade
And relief from the heat
Where little birds retreat
For security in their haven of rest,
And to build their little nests.
When daylight is ending
    and colors are blending,
What a blessing to me
When every color of the rainbow I can see,
As the sun comes blazing through the trees,
And my vibrations say the Lord
    is well-pleased.

Time

Shadows are shifting
      as minute by minute,
           time becomes a non-entity.
When comes next the breaking of dawn,
      time becomes propinquity,
As creation begins to spawn.

Then, in juxtaposition,
      society becomes a decadent state,
With endless time in which to relate.
'Tis right about now that time should march on,
But due to relativity,
      it's just about gone!

Talking to the Moon

In awesome wonder,
    I looked up at you,
Wondering what on earth
    one such as I could do
To show my gratitude.

I watched as you were waxing,
And now that you are waning,
    such thoughts I'm
        entertaining
(as you are passing by):

  "Did you strew those
  twinkling lights as
  you strolled
    across the sky?"

The Active Little Leaf

That lone little leaf, hanging up there,
Twisting and turning, and flapping in the air—
So persistently insistent,
    it leaves the world pass by,
Without even heaving a nostalgic sigh.
Now all other leaves are calling it a day,
And long since, they've all been on their way—
Down to the ground
In a loosely-piled mound,
To facilitate silly people who rake them around.
But this little leaf says, "Go if you wish,"
And then with a dip and a frivolous swish,
"I'll stay as I am,
as long as I can."
So twisting and twirling, she spends each day,
Unconcernedly waiting for come what may.

The Baby Oak Tree

My baby oak tree grows and grows.
Where 'twill stop, no one knows.
Before it got a start,
'Twas most broken in part,
By a motorist who hadn't a care
About people or plants treasured so rare.
By the time it recovered from this,
And life was becoming with bliss,
Along comes a clod on a big old truck,
And begins to run things amuck!

Before I could stop him, he pulled and he twisted,
Not caring whether my tree existed.
It was several months this time
Before the tree could ever climb
Back to the height where it had been before.
Now I'm watching and waiting
      and hopefully keeping score.

The Bounty

The golden glow of the west
Is sunset at its best—
With this view I am blessed.
Each day that's devoid of rain,
Spectacular riches I gain,
And then a glorious experience
      comes into view
As beginnings of dawn
      start to ensue,
With the moon up high,
When Venus is nigh,
A bounty I spy
As the heavenly body
      puts electric lights to shame,
While, forever, it glows with fame,
As the No. 1 Stellar, in name.
What a blessing by right of birth,
To be a part of this creation
      called earth!

The Breeze and the Trees

The understanding between the wind and the leaves
Is a relation that a poet perceives.
    There's a soulful vibration
        instigated by creation
In the beginning ages of time—
    eons of periods of prime
Miracles to be promoted
        by sages anciently emoted
Into captivity of enshrouded well-being,
Giving rise to the flow of life's freeing
Of the beginning magnetics of the growth of the trees,
As reaching out, they capture the breeze.

The Cedarwood Heart
(In Memory of a Childhood Sweetheart)

'Twas under a huckleberry tree
You made a promise to me
That you would ever faithful be.
You carved me a cedarwood heart,
With which I ne'er shall part,
Albeit, ever, come what may—
And although you went away
(to return too late another day).
There's always love to impart,
Locked away with a little cedar heart.

The Coming of the Green

The Coming of the Green
    is a season, supreme,
When the coolness of the light
    in the forest, so pristine,
Casts mystic shadows of tall trees,
    shortening and lengthening,
        as nature decrees,
Providing relief in the heat of day,
    as nature's creatures pass this way.
Then just about daylight, when temperature drops,
The creeping and crawling of nature stops.
Big trees offer ample protection
    as each little creature
        makes his selection
For a place to hide during daylight hours,
    up tree trunks and among the bowers.
And this is how nature has its way
    of distinguishing the night
        from the day.

The Eagle's Prey

As I was going for my walk,
I heard sweet birdie talk.
'Twas the top of a morn in May—
For a stroll, a perfect day.

I saw an eagle soaring high—
Almost touching the sky!
To his mate, he cried:
"Oh, a prey, I do spy!
On my catch, you must rely.

"So heat up the water—
      sharpen up the knife,
And a feast, we'll have,
      my little sweet wife!"

For such things, I was listening,
      while walking very slow,
It's that I understand bird talk,
      don't you know?

The Enchanting Storm

How enchanting is the movement
    of the leaves
        on the trees,
And o'erwhelming is realization
    that I see
        what God decrees.

As now a storm approaches,
    I must take my pad and quill,
        and as severity encroaches,
            I'll not relax until
My excitement has been sated,
    and breathelessness abated,
        through beauty of God's will.

Now darkness is o'ertaking
    all the brightness o'er the hill,
        and violent winds
            have become now still,
While thunder roars its mighty strength
    to limits of sound's length,
Frightening all God's creatures
    in their life's race
        to find a hiding place,

Avoiding as they flee,
    what might've been to be,
Had they, themselves, remained exposed
    to lightning (death transposed)!

The Fennel and the Goldenrod

The animated fennel in the soft autumn breeze,
Waved to Miss Goldenrod, up near the tall trees.
Says she:
    "My dear friend,
    an ear to me, please lend.
    I've an idea to convey
    if you listen and obey.
    Please permit me to you urge
    that together we might merge
    your glorious golden color
       with my soft and silent ways,
    that we might share the beauty
       of these longed-for heavenly days.
    If we could get together
    in some very suitable weather,
    there might be a mutation,
    in essence, a creation,
    of some rare, unusual plant,
    that, in name, God would grant
    a permanent life of beauty—
    to grow here through self-duty
    to plant and animal life,
    where we pray for no more strife."

The Three Fennels

There were three fennels standing by the way.
The little one in the middle had much to say:
"Mommie, why have you turned so gold?
Is it because you're getting old?

"Daddy and I are still very green,
And my antics in the breeze are much to be seen,
Twisting and swaying while conversing with you—
What more can a little one be expected to do?"

"There's quite a story, my precious babe,"
She explained, as in the gentle breeze she swayed.
"We were once living on a distant farm,
Way back a ways from either hurt or harm—
Back behind an old, old barn,

"Where cows and other beings disturbed not our peace,
And on everyday life we had a permanent lease.
But then, in moves this active pair
Who would spy on us in our little lair.

"So admiring were they of our silken beauty—
To preserve us, they thought, was their appointed duty.
In autumn their many long breaths were bated,
As for perfection in harvest time they waited.

"When the north winds began to turn cold,
Our shimmery greenery became burnished gold.
Then here comes the lady, big knife in hand,
And cuts us down, every stand—

"Packed in a sack, we were hauled away,
To wherever (we thought, come what may)—
And scattered, were we, on a run-down field.
Where 'twould be a questionable amount of yield.

"But here we are, the three of us—
Our health and energy, near a plus.
Who knows what's in store for us from here?
Take patience and wait for another year."

The Fiddling Man

There's a dear old fiddling man
Who's the best one in the land.
And when he plays that thing,
You can hear the angels sing.

Like the touch of the master's hand,
Notes will answer his command—
Like voices sweet and low,
He drags out with that bow.

You can hear the hound dogs baying
While the "Fox Chase" he is playing.
Then the next thing you are knowing,
That old rooster starts a-crowing,

"And the old hen cackles,
    she cackles on the lot.
But the next time she cackles,
    she'll cackle in the pot."

When he gets up on that stage
(Despite his years in age),
The old fellow still plays well;
Music vibrates like a bell.

And when he gets Up There,
You can hear him loud and clear,
Playing "Turkey in the Straw,"
Without even one little flaw.

Angels' accompaniment they will bring
By the flutter of their wings,
With much glory and grace to share,
Giving to all with loving care.
   (*A Christmas gift in dedication to author's fiddling
         brother, Everis Campbell*)

The Final Glory

Little bits of color, showing through my balcony door,
Are only small samples of what nature has in store
In all great wonders, way out yonder,
Bringing rapturous blessings, with which to ponder,
Albeit struggles through myriad adversities
    of constant daily controversies.
From our Temple of God, we see beauty through His
   eyes
      as only we can surmise.

How I crave power of peace,
      giving God control of my life through lease
Of a lifetime existence,
      through my own persistence.
God grant me the grace of constant prayer
In asking for blessings, one day at a time—
For achievement of the final glory, sublime!

The General and the Private

Comes solutions
    (naught sans the ablutions)—
For meeting requirements
   of early morning troop inspection.
As a modification, 'twas an interesting collection.
They had gone to the extreme
For a state of polished gleam,
When out walks Private Brown;
    his hat was a crown,
With garlands of daisies, gathered all around.
His rifle he was dragging,
    along across the ground.
"What meaning is this, Sergeant?"
    the Inspector General bellowed!
"I'm sure there's an explanation, Sir"
    (The Sergeant's tone was calm
       and mellowed).
When quizzed, the young private replied
    (as penitently he cried):
"Oh, Sir, I picked the flowers there
    for your lady's beautiful hair—
On my hat I placed them then,
    so they could have some air."
In a voice husky with emotion,
    the Inspector General shouted:
"Deliver the flowers, Private, to my lady, fair,
And as you bear them to her,
    handle them with care!"

The Glory of Shadows

'Tis but 'twas there just for me,
Only the shadow of a tree—
A reflection on the side of a wall
    in glorious green,
As if flashed upon a screen,
Epitomizing grandeur of nature
    at its best,
As painted by the Master's hand
    at His behest.
Let me scribble while I can,
Before the magic leaves my hand—
Imaginary things of a mind so bold,
Which comes natural to a poet so old!

The Good Old Days

Stately and supreme
      stood the great oak, serene,
By the way of the road
Where one could tote the weary load
To the cotton house across the open field.
'Twas a year that brought the heavy yield,
For to buy the things so dear,
Like for Christmas and good cheer;
For school books by the stack
That kids slung across their back
In a unique container made from a flour sack.
These have been called the good old days
But, to me, there are different ways
To reach maturity
      in a satisfactory state of security.

The Gypsy Violinist

Mournful sounds of a violin's cry,
With the hush of a sweet lullaby,
Brought back a stirring refrain
From memories he must regain.

Standing with his heart on his sleeve,
He played as if trying to reprieve
A lost love somewhere in the past—
Why, oh, why couldn't it last?

Observing the tears on his face,
To enfold him in my embrace
Would be all of fate I could ask—
As if God had made it my task.

Soft, muted notes of haunting strains
Of music in my memory remains—
Thoughts of love, long ago lost!
Oh, come back to me, at any cost!

Play on, dear Gypsy Man—
Sweetest music in all the land!

The Lady and Her Flute

There sounded a rapturous beat
Of sweet notes, beginning now to retreat,
in a low moaning wail,
from a flute, to prevail,
as the leader of the band
(well-known across the land)
now steps out, in all her elegance,
renewing the beat, in all its prevalence,
telling the world, with a flashing smile,
it's likely to take her quite awhile
to bring to the audience heartfelt emotion,
expressed with all her deepest devotion.
To all the world, dedicated was she,
in sharing her glory, as meant to be—
Synonymous with music was her every feeling.
In her soulful outlet, 'twas most appealing
as a poet, expressing in every line,
music to match
vibrations sublime!

The Little Fennel Seed

(Swaying in the breeze),
    "Tell me, if you please,
      how it came to be that
        I'm here among the trees?"
    "Well, to the best of my knowledge
      (despite my lack of college),
'twas from a little seed,"
    said the taller fennel weed.
"Now, a family of three,
    we're happy as can be—
If you'll listen for a spell,
some genealogy I will tell—
In the poem coming up next,
to be found in this same context."

The Little Switch Tree
and
What It Grew Up to Be

A switch of a tree, never meant to be
In such a close and crowded space,
From the beginning, should have been
      in another place,
But the squirrel who planted it
      had a reason why—
Visions, had he, 'twould grow to the sky.
Said one big tree, "Why not form a conspiracy?
Spread your leaves, Great Mr. Oak,
      so wide she cannot see
The sun, nor even the bow of the rain,
'Way over there, across the plain.
Lie down and die, you little dwarf,
      from non-importancy!
You'll never amount to anything,
      for nothing you'll ever be!"
In a period of time, the little one grew up—
      in fact, much higher than the others
(the spurning ones, her older brothers).
From the tip of her top, Little Tree looks down
On the jealous branches, drooping toward the ground.
"See," says she, "just look at me!
Higher than ever I was meant to be.
Supporting, I am, to the squirrel's family.
I'm up here with my procreator,
In nature's own amphitheater."

The Lonely Tree

Forlorn and lonely stood the tree—
Many a time did it remind me of me,
All alone, without hope,
Ne'er one day was it able to cope

With adversities and disease
And very little breeze
From which relief to gain
When there's very little rain.

There was dust from plowed fields,
With nothing for a shield—
Not even little plants—
Just mean old fire ants,
And its roots they did devour
While life for it turned sour.

Now it's just an old stump
Standing there, alone, in a lump.
For this tree no life of magic—
Just one long era, most tragic.

The Mangled Little Oak

There's a mangled little oak
  with aspen-looking bark,
Standing so forlorn and all alone,
  looking very stark.
Among the rest of the trees,
  she's a mere cull,
And but for little birds,
  her life would be dull.
A group of tiny ones on their flight,
  passing through,
Looking for bugs, stop to pick a few
Among her broken, dead branches
  (torn by the storm),
Which ravages of time
  have left looking worn.
But God has his way of bringing
  ways about
To feed little creatures—
  surely, there's no doubt
That the ragged little tree
  without any clout,
Stands with open arms
  to welcome little birds,
Bringing all their charms,
  their singing galore,
And multiplying by the score.

The Master's Brush

One more day God granted me
The beauty of a sunset to see.
With my lack of ability to describe
The strokes of a brush once applied
By the greatest artist of all time,
In all of His omnipotence, sublime,
Could I but just once from the sky pluck
The beauty no camera has ever struck!
The colors now are fading
     from this glorious view,
And tiny clouds cascading—
       daylight, they subdue.

The Mighty Storm

O mighty storm!
I've loved these trees since I was born!
The splendor you bring as you twist and roll
The high treetops, arranged as a scroll,
Swishing among clouds scurrying past
While capturing sunbeams sufficient to last
In support of power as lightning has flashed.
I could watch forever, these manifestations—
Awesomely enraptured with admiration!
Oh, pray, great storm, don't take my tallest tree,
For its thrilling performances
are meant just for me!

The Mills of the Gods

And the mills of the gods, slowly they turned,
grinding as they burned
from friction, no less,
while the sands of time
passed fast,
cooling, as they merged with the streams of life,
along life's byways. And highways.

The Old Ghost Town

Starlights are twinkling o'er the old ghost town.
Days there were when in yore, lights were low down.
Laughter was light,
    while music played softly way into the night.
Here and there a guitar was strummed
    while lilting laughter hummed,
As full-skirted damsels charmed the men some more,
Making fantastic patterns as they whirled around the
    floor.
One has but to meditate and reminisce to recreate
Those days of long ago
    when life was one big show.

The Orange Rose

Thank you, God, that I can see
The beauty Thou hast wrought for me.
Never in my experience has a phenomenon like this
Brought the power of such glory, unequaled in bliss.

So majestic and tall,
It scales the wall,
To heights of adulation,
The fairest in all creation!

Such beauty unexcelled,
Graceful head on high, upheld
By its proudness to be
Manifesting, Lord, to Thee!

To an Orange Rose

Ne'er such beauty has the Creator wrought
As the wondrous glow of the Orange Rose.
By culturists much sought,
And comparable in class to the music of Bose.

The willowy rose sways in the breeze,
While hummingbirds hum to the drone of bumblebees.
Diamonds sparkling in the dew,
Bless an early morning view.

With the grace of a queen,
Height stately supreme,
On grass and leaves, with care,
She spreads her perfume, rare.

How, with uncertainties of spring,
Can priceless petals cling?
For photos rare, make haste.
There's no time to waste.

The Last Orange Rose

There she stands in all her beauty,
Looking to the clouds from ten feet in the air.
Stately and tall, 'tis her only duty,
To grace the world and show her care

And wonderful phenomena of glory,
Defying all adversity to bring us the story
Of the beauteous existence of summer's last rose,
More heavenly in nature than anyone knows.

Many years now in existence, this unique orange
    blessing
Absorbing nature's strength, her petals caressing
The beak of the hummingbird high on the wing,
And bumblebees droning, as pollen they bring.

Growing taller each year, to reach the sky,
Where angel wings compete with bees and birds, by
    and by,
For the attentions of one so special, to enter infinity,
Fading into nonexistence, with complete anonymity.

The Old Oak Tree Above the Eaves

The gleam
    of the sheen
        of the glimmering leaves
Of the old oak tree
    above the eaves
Of the cottage underneath the trees,
Brought inspiration to me
        that I thought was never to be.
The beauty I viewed, 'twas like painted on a screen—
        the likes of which I'd never seen.
This pallet and brush
    exceed Michelangelo
To heights of which no one can aspire
    from so far down below.
I'll stay as I am,
        thanking God I still can,
            to appreciate the work
    of a master artist who
        doesn't shirk!

The Power of Reflection

Sitting between windows
    that face the east and the west,
'Tis hard to perceive
    that I can receive
Two phenomena in my quest,
    to be doubly blest!
To the west, above the horizon,
Bursting forth so brilliantly bright
    (I can hardly keep my eyes on)—
Diamonds! Sparkling in every direction!
Across the world to the east, in reflection,
On magnificent colors in stately oaks
    and sweetgum trees,
Which are gently swaying in the breeze,
As they whisper to their leaves:
    "We are universal in perfection—
    We can travel east to west
    at a moment's direction,
    by Reflection!"

The Ruby in the Sky

There's a sparkling gem
      in the northwest—
To its spectacular beauty
      can I attest.
Each day at this time,
      I sit and wait,
For fear that I will miss
      (if I am late)
Every color of the rainbow,
      shown in every hue,
By this ruby in the sky,
      with such a gorgeous view.
Now I know that You are watching
      from the place wherever You are;
Dear Lord, please say how far
      from yon distant star.
Omnipotence, may it be Thy will
      that I gaze from on this hill
Toward Your mighty feats of grace—
      miracles with Thine every pace.
Please, O God, give me the faith,
      each circumstance, to appreciate.

The Scribbler

'Tis off to "land of nod" for me,
For it's awake I'll be
At a quarter of three.
For an hour or so, I'll be a poet—
Reams, I'll scribble before you know it!

If in rhythm I could coax my body to change,
To others then, I mightn't seem so strange.
I'll pull my blinds and close them tight—
So maybe they'll think I sleep all night.

God gave me this talent and He understands.
So why should I cater to others' demands?
With my Savior, I can always share
All life's secrets and emotions, rare.

The Sounds of Night

Oh, how I love the sounds of night,
When all little creatures sing outright—
Their voices unthrottled and coats unfurled,
Telling their stories to the world.

The owl gives a hoot
     and a shriek, to boot,
While the dog gives a howl
     to accompany the owl.
Now comes the squirrel across the roof,
Friskily prancing—not so aloof!

The whippoorwill trills
     across the hills
And life goes along
     with the merriest song,
All through the night,
     As I pick up my pen
And begin to write!

The Story in My Heart

Deep inside the chambers
    of each part
      of my heart
Lies the answer to the mystery
    of the innards of my soul—
A story that remains forever untold.
Being not what 'twas once thought,
'Tis, of further use, now naught
That the answer should be sought,
    another day,
    come what may—
Thus my riddle may be solved
As same questions are revolved.

The Sun Bids Adieu

Bedazzling, to say the least—
By the moment, colors increase.
The sun bids adieu
As it rapidly fades from view.

And the night falls, in submission,
To fulfill its commission—
Imprisoned in darkness,
And overwhelmed by starkness

The long hours through
(Albeit refreshed by dew),
Before the morning view
Of the sun comes once again
When it will ascend.

The Touch of His Hand

Angel hair across the sky
      one more coat should He apply?
As it is, let it stand—
      'tis the touch of the Master's hand.
The sky is so blue,
      in the shade that's true—
Essence of grandeur is in perfection,
      a favorite in the Master's collection
Of created things
      for earth that He brings
To people both great and small,
      no matter as to accomplishments, at all,
It seems,
      but, by all means,
'Tis our God-given duty
      to thank Him for the beauty
With which we are blest
      at His behest.

The Unawakened Forest

In the shadows of the deep
Lies a forest half asleep,
With many treasures unfound,
And mythical secrets, most profound.

Who knows what scientists, there, could find
If they'd only half a mind
To probe in places undisturbed,
Where once-intended work was curbed,

Procrastinating till another day,
Hoping for less effort to find, would they.
Now more boost we seek to borrow,
In the hopes of a coming morrow.

The Wise Old Oak

A wondrous giant oak stood
In the denseness of the wood.
All alone for a century was she,
And greater in wisdom than any other tree.

Many creatures were sheltered by her branches
As the rains came pouring in avalanches.
And thousands of diamonds sparkled like dew,
Encompassed with beauty as the sun shone through.

Big ripe acorns she would drop for the squirrel,
Watching him leap as his tail he'd unfurl.
She could sense the approach (by the song that he sang)
Of the dear whippoorwill and his notes as they rang:
      "Chip the widow's redoak."

Who knows how many rings are in this great tree,
Or what age in years she is meant to be?
The wise old owl, usually so moot,
Replied (when asked), that he didn't give a hoot!

The Unveiling
Dedicated to Thomas Kinkade

Portrayed, was a panoramic review
      of serenity in its entirety—
A spectacular array of art to ensue
In all its splendor and propriety.
'Twould surpass all other things of import,
Things worthy of day's events to report.
The atmosphere was imbued
      with enchantment, serene,
As appreciation of beauty, purviewed,
By the crowd in silence, supreme.

Hushed, was the stillness—
      the moment of waiting
For removal of cover from the canvas,
      When time has arrived
for celebrating.
So great were his accomplishments—
      The Hall of Fame
      He did attain
From ethereal beauty portrayed
By an artist so great—Thomas Kinkade!

The Voice of Silence

In the quiet of the peace of silence,
There is much to be learned at night.
As I listen to the voice of silence,
Much of time do I ponder my plight.

Listen to the voice of silence!
Stories of ages long told,
You'll hear shelves of old,
Beckoning you to come listen—

As from ages of dust they arise
From memories long since gone,
And you sit there in reverie, all alone,
Wishing for transition, back to then.

The Whole World a Canvas

Imagine the entire universe
    a canvas of robin's-egg blue,
Dappled all over with blobs of eiderdown,
    of a rose and gray hue!

Now I know why I was kept here so long—
I am sure everybody can hear my heartstrings
    twanging a song!
None are the most ancient sages
    who could describe what I saw today—
Nor brushes of famous painters,
    such as Angelo or Monet.

The whole world was aglow,
    with a gorgeous galactic show.
Naught words of description are there,
    to portray a picture, fair,
Of the permanent visual imprint
    of a spectacular sunset view
That is etched forever in my heart
    for a jumpstart,
To start it over anew!

The Wonderful Field of Medicine

In the field of medicine, lies much hope
For the sick and the weak, via inimitable scope.
Frequently, there are hopeless advanced cases,
Wherein the Master, with an angel, embraces
The flow of knowledge with which His emissary is imbued,
Using every technique great learning has accrued.
The blessings of ability, understanding, and compassion,
all embodied in one,
Were presented to one in need, along with an aura,
Wreathing a smile, bright as the sun!

Things Unforetold

Gold reflections on the wall
    cast through trees so great and tall,
Changing patterns with the breeze,
    through swaying branches of the trees.
'Twas as if a higher being,
    His brushes lifted, as if seeing
Potential of a great sensation,
    recorded by a spiritual creation.
Wistful breezes sigh
    through wispy clouds on high,
Telling a story of things unforetold,
    by ancient Sages, oh, so old!

Thoughts from Afar

'Twas a harbinger of good will—
Sounds coming from o'er the hill,
Borne by winds of fate,
And heard before too late—
Brought back from thoughts afar,
Like a wondrous, distant star,
Suspended by who knows what?
Or is it there, or is it not?
Extant one moment, but gone the next—
The whole conjecture is out of context.

Thwarted Realms of Time

Submerged in being forever more,
From the very depths of my soul,
Thwarted realms of time unfold,
In rhymes of music, poetry, and lore.

Turn not back, pages to restore.
'Tis only a short distance to yon shore,
From where the time is standing still—
From where, aft then, is no more nil.

'Tis crost old River Styx, enraged and boiling,
That God's angels assist the acquitted in their foiling
Of attempts by Satan's angels to add another cry
To the clamor of the helpless as they go writhing by.

Timeless Beauty

    I stare with inspiration at the old cultivator,
Placed by the hands of a great innovator.
    I stand by my window, stricken with awe,
As to how time and beauty can mend each flaw,
    Of the wobbly old wheels of such rich-colored rust,
Covered in green vines and showered with dust.
    There's so much beauty in ugly to be seen,
Looking in the right place, at the right scene.

Time for Rest

Beyond words or measure,
Are the splendorous treasures
Displayed by nature's glory—
'Tis a rapturous story.

Let me live, O Lord,
    to the end of this season.
To end for me such beauty,
    would be without reason.
And I know 'twould not be planned
    for there to be such waste,
My time being already
    so well-paced.

Let me look without stopping
    till the end of each day,
Lest some beauty I might miss
    in an instantaneous moment
        just one glance away.

Out my window, I'll be looking
Upon this panoramic view;
And with each change of color,
I'll perceive a picture, new.

There will come a day when I cannot see;[*]
I wish 'twere so, 'tis not to be.
'Tis then will end my constant quest,
It being then the time to rest!

[*]Approaching blindness from Macular Degeneration

To Each His Own

How miraculously we grow
    with passage of time,
        as we come to know
The sweetness of life,
        as God's generous gift
To each, his own, setting sails adrift—
Each on to his predestined
    windward direction,
Perhaps to seek his fortune
        through some remote connection.
Who knows where or when
        each journey must end?

To Forever Abide

When I'm feeling most alone,
A Presence to which I atone,
O'er me, keeps watch
      through the night—
In realms of glory, shining bright.
As I place my trust to His care,
My burdens He will ever bear.

Leave me not, O Savior of mine—
Happiness with Thee, I opine.
Pray ne'er shall I leave Thy side—
Forever with me, shalt Thou abide.

To Fulfill Unfinished Efforts

O God, I most humbly beseech Thy Grace.
If be it that earth services should be my pace,
Use me in whatever way that I may
Please Thine Omnipotence, I pray,
That I, with my humble approach,
Might inspire others to take my place,
To carry on descriptions
      of what nature has wrought—
To fulfill unfinished efforts
      with beauty that's sought.
God, grant me the privilege
      of establishing preservation
Through wishes to give
      a great inspiration,
And bring forth in this age,
      a great innovation.
God bless every minute
      of an artistry in creation.

To Like the Eagle, Be

In the still of the night,
Through the cry of my violin,
Oh, the tales I could spin!
And the sounds I would mute
With the moans of my flute!

Now to pick up the pace—
Let syncopated rhythm embrace
Every sound that's featured
Through persistence
In timeless existence.

"Come, little owls, and sing with me!
Let out your notes, wild and free!"
My freedom of spirit, released
Through music, undaunted
By the sigh of breeze
Through the trees,
Is flaunted.

Like the soaring of an eagle,
Higher and higher—
A feathered, free flyer.
Oh, would that my spirit
Could be set free—
To like the eagle, be!

To Paint a Word Picture

Had I but one day left to see
The beauty created for me,
'Tis painted sufficiently
By the touch of the Master's hand,
For as long as the world shall stand.
In all the days long since,
And all to come forth hence,
Never to compare are they
With the beauty of this one day.
Thank God for sufficient vision left
(That it's not totally bereft),
To view nature in all its glory.
Could I but tell the full story
In poetic terms of inspiration,
Bringing to life a spiritual vibration.
Would I were in a class with Shelley and Keats—
I could paint a word picture (with no repeats)
Of the beauty of feathery wisps floating by,
Against a background of blue, blue sky,
And the sparkling of leaves as they lazily sway
On the trees,
    from the breeze,
On this wonderful spring day.

Tree and Bird Story

Telling a colorful story,
The small sweetgum, in awesome glory,
Stands as always it has been,
Outside my window in the glen.

Through many a fickle season,
Its tolerance could find small reason
For such a long drouth,
Albeit the South

Is noted for weather extremes.
How one follows the other, is beyond wildest dreams!
Yesterday the tree was dying of thirst;
Today come rain clouds, the biggest one, first

To quench this part of the valley—
Oh, see how the birds do rally!
They keep their wings dry,
Lest naught may they fly

Up North, where the weather is cool,
To dip their feet in the pool
By the house of the lady, old,
Who for them will bread, mold,

In the light of the early morn,
From meal she made of corn
And the wheat which she will grind
For bread of its own kind.

Now in the winter the birds return;
Good old South they do not spurn,
To tell about their travels, to the sweetgum tree,
And of how generous a dear old lady can be.

Two Proud Little Leaves

Two little "eyes" stared back at me,
From down in the woods,
    through a half-concealed tree.
It was two small leaves who had lost their green
    but (to their delight)
    could still be seen.
They were surrounded by ones still very much alive,
Who had no concern about how to survive.
But the dark of their color, enhanced by twilight,
Absorbed (rather than reflected) the fast-fading light.
Now that is the story of how two dead leaves
Once outshone the live ones, and were very much
    pleased!

Unacclaimed Lines

The jade of the green is my opening scene
To the scenario of a wild dream.
As I stare out my window of wonders,
Lest more than enough, my mind could ponder,
I must turn to more thoughts of the day
as needs must could say,
Lest too much of my time I am tempted to squander,
My pen I grab up to describe wonder of wonders.
Hurry to sit, and all lines I have writ
Are scenarios of dreams—
Where sunbeam and moonbeam
Alternately gleam while I dream
Through the day, to hasten my way
Toward attainment of one more poem, sublime—
As much acclaimed as "Ages of Time!"

Undulating Patterns

Had I only the artist's touch
    to portray patterns on the wall,
Created there by nature—
    the greatest master of all!

A cool background of pastel serenity,
    sans possible marks of obscenity,
Is enshrouded by shadows, en masse,
    obliquely arranged, with convoluted strata
        of movement, non-crass.

Unique are manifestations of shadows so animated,
Leaving to the imagination how 'twas all created,
In this strange quandary, held fast!

Unfinished Endeavors

Of things literary,
So afraid am I to carry
To my grave, half-spent,
Ideas of good intent,
Which to me, in days of yore,
Were of import to me no more.

I'll hitch my team to spirits high,
And I shall get there by and by—
Up where, for me, there's only peace,
And on my life there is no lease.

For my work to finish,
May I relinquish
All unimportant childish thoughts
And many other things of naught—

That I may gain in glorious grace,
For God's approval to embrace
My endeavors to reach the place
Where I can look upon His face.

Unmended Fences

'Tis getting near the end
And the fences, one can't mend.
Turn not back the clocks of time—Nay!

Nor can one recall mistakes that have been made.
It's too late now
      to make a vow
That all originalities
      shall not have been decayed.

'Tis not so easy that this page of life be turned,
And naught, anon, should ever it be burned.

Neither, as we turn,
      will it go away—
Alas! As of now,
      it is there to stay!

Voices in the Wind

So smoothly go voices as they blend
Together, as they're talking in the wind.
      Harmony so sweet,
Sounding through notes so very fleet—
Strains of a violin's soft cry,
So appealing that angels must comply,
In a medley of satin notes on strings.
Echoes from the heart the Master brings,
Wrenching the very depths of an artist's soul,
Hopefully reaching for realms of treasures, untold.

Wayward Winds

Like ocean waves, tree tops are rolling,
And wailing winds, like heartstrings, extolling,
Through dark density on mountainous walls,
Where torrents of water, as the rain falls,
Roar along in cadence with the whistle of the winds,
Waiting not for responses that its echo sends,
As notes, so creative, into a tune blends,
Bringing peace to a soul, so tossed about
(By pangs of misery that it cannot rout).
Listen to the wind, oh, voices of my mind—
Thereby (through deep thought) serenity to find!

Window View of Beauty

The jading of the green, providing a background, serene,
Enhances a window view of greenery o'er the hill,
Emphasized by the mocking bird's sweet trill.
An early morning sunbeam's kiss
Of freshness emanates an aura of bliss,
Surrounding universal beauty all around—
Dissolution of encapsulated eminence, profound—
Wrought by the Master's own hand,
And distributed at His command!

Wishful Dreams of Heaven

Oh let these sweet birds be.
Friends, they are, to come to me.
Happiness to me, they will bring,
Sitting on my shoulder, with me, to sing.
Of all creatures in heaven, birds are most divine—
Midst dearest of earth memories, birds are sublime.
Their notes so inspiring
Early of morn, it seems they are conspiring
As to which melody they'll use
To announce the break of day.
But to try as they may,
'Tis all played by ear.
Heavenly location could ne'er be more near.
And with my friend birds,
To me it's now occurred
That I'll see my Darling Koni,
Little Flower of the wild,
With spirit not so mild.
To bring her breakfast goodies
Is the joy of my day!
And to tell how much I love her
Is more than I can say!
In this great imagination
I'm beginning to see
Just how wonderful heaven can be.

Wonderful Wonders

Wonderful are the wonders
Of this mystic, wonderful world.
For me, as I wander,
Endless beauty is unfurled.
In all of its grandiloquence
(sans indefinite exploration),
Myriad sites of great creation
Stand unviewed among the crowd—
Albeit sought, success but naught.
Weep not that you've missed the best
(east to east, or west to west)—
'tis only that when you return,
More esoteric, you'll discern
Difference in the chaff and grain—
To ne'er more need come back again.

Wonderful Words of Rhyme

Encapsulated dust and mosses of age—
Long since passed time, page by page.
Prepared not for passage, those pages of time,
Lying lifeless and still, in silent opine.
Oh, to bring back activity so great!
New emotions to instill or reinstate—
'Twould be heavenly reflections from above,
Of what can be wrought on wings of love!
Come back to me, oh, waves of inspiration,
From the dust bins of time.
Bring a new creation of precious words, sublime.
May I have the ability of great contribution,
In the world of poetry, for a new constitution!
Ridding our shelves of words, unblended
that crowd our space with collections unintended.
I am asking from the greatest sage of all time,
The power to bring back poetry, divine—
To sweep clean the places for creations so fine,
In perpetuation for scribblers of verses that rhyme!

Words Gone Adrift

Oh, but for words to describe this view,
A treasure in pastels, to paint, I would pursue
    were I an artist, true.
As clouds are increasing,
    for fear a storm will brew,
I find myself groping
    for words to accrue
Ways of apt portrayal
    befitting nature's gift
Before, perhaps in weather,
    there comes a rift.
Lord, help me recapture
    my words gone adrift,
For it seems that my memory
    of words is now bereft.
I'll write as I remember,
    phrases sweet and tender,
To continue thus until
    no longer this arrangement
Meets my Lord's will.

Yearning for Learning

For a higher learning,
One should never stop yearning.
Reach for a place high up with the stars,
Be it ever so very far.

Perhaps one day—
Who can say—
You'll be glad you did,
When it's time for your last bid.